Belles-Lettres

Writings of Hijab Imtiaz Ali
With Foreword by Haider Shahbaz

Edited and Translated from Urdu by

SASCHA A. AKHTAR

OXFORD
UNIVERSITY PRESS

Oxford University Press is a department of the University of Oxford.
It furthers the University's objective of excellence in research, scholarship,
and education by publishing worldwide. Oxford is a registered trade mark of
Oxford University Press in the UK and in certain other countries

Published in India by
Oxford University Press
22 Workspace, 2nd Floor, 1/22 Asaf Ali Road, New Delhi 110002, India

© Oxford University Press India 2022

The moral rights of the author have been asserted

Third impression 2023

ISBN-13 (Paperback): 978-0-19-013264-4
ISBN-10 (Paperback): 0-19-013264-7

ISBN-13 (Digital-Online (OSO)): 978-9-35-497497-7
ISBN-10 (Digital-Online (OSO)): 9-35-497497-X

ISBN-13 (eBook): 978-9-35-497496-0
ISBN-10 (eBook): 9-35-497496-1

DOI: 10.1093/oso/9780190132644.001.0001

Typeset in Minion Pro 10/13
by Newgen Knowledge Works Pvt. Ltd.
Printed at Repro India Limited

Dedicated to the family of Hijab Imtiaz Ali Taj and to all of us, partitioned who feel robbed of our own culture. Here is a piece of the literary puzzle that is us.

Acknowledgements

The translator owes a debt of gratitude to the work of Aamer Hussein in illuminating the writings of women writers from the Subcontinent and his translations of *Adab-E-Zareen* in various journals including *Asymptote*. I also thank Aamer for being there in the early stages to unlock some of the mysteries. I thank my agent Kanishka Gupta for believing in the importance of the project and all the poets, authors, fellow translators, students, academics, who have expressed great enthusiasm for wanting to read this book. They have patiently waited over the years that it has taken to reach this point, as have my comrades from Pakistan who were equally enchanted to learn about Hijab Imtiaz and the translation of *Adab-E-Zareen*.

Thank you to my nana, Haq Nawaz Akhtar, with whom I got to share some of the translations and the news of this work just before he left this world. The memories of sitting on a charpai and reading to him after his stroke are ones I cherish. I also thank Shoaib Sultan Khan, whose invaluable advice on certain Urdu words helped me proceed.

I am so grateful to Yasmine and Nadeem Tahir, for welcoming me into their home to speak of their dear Bibi, Hijab Imtiaz, and share with me the many anecdotes. That time was one that I shall never forget.

Above all, I thank the Arts Council England for supporting me whilst I was working on the book and allowing me to travel to conduct research in Lahore. It is such support for the work of South Asians that fosters real change, and has far-reaching implications.

Hijab Imtiaz Ali
An Avant-Garde Romantic

Haider Shahbaz

In her collection of autobiographical essays, *Kaghazi Hai Pairahan*, the famous Urdu progressive writer, Ismat Chugtai, recounts travelling to Lahore
in the early forties to attend the court proceedings regarding the charge of
obscenity on her afsana, *Lihaaf*. She meets many different writers in Lahore
during this winter trip, including Hijab Imtiaz Ali.

Her description of Hijab Imtiaz's countenance is pithy: *kuch udaas, kuch
roothi* ('a little melancholy, a little sullen' in Naqvi and Memon's translation).
The first thing she observes is the excessive amount of make-up Hijab Imtiaz
is wearing—'tons of Kajal'. Then she mentions that she seems lost in her own
thoughts and uninterested in conversation. Perhaps, Chugtai says, she is lost
in 'the very atmosphere that gushes from her pen like a puff of imaginary
smoke and weaves a rainbow-colored shell around her'. Chugtai's friend, the
iconic writer, Manto, who is accompanying her, is even less generous. He
simply declares Hijab Imtiaz 'a fraud'.

Chugtai's observations are unkind, but unsurprising. A sharp and com-
mitted realist, arguably the finest progressive and feminist writer Urdu
has ever produced, Chugtai could not hide her unfavourable view of Hijab
Imtiaz's romanticism. She wanted to unveil the harsh realities Muslim
women experienced instead of embellishing them with a 'puff of imaginary
smoke' or encasing them in a 'rainbow-coloured shell'.

The reception of Hijab's work—from the mid-20th century to our contemporary moment—as quintessentially romantic seems to be shaped
by critics to fit a convenient biographical mould of a snooty, escapist, and
frivolous woman writer. There is no doubt that Hijab Imtiaz's early stories
of comic and tragic love affairs set in picturesque locations and published
in women's magazines earned her incredible fame and a devoted readership. But looking at her work retrospectively, we also see many other types
of writing: collections of horror stories; propagandistic diary entries from
times of war; novels based on psychoanalytic theories; and towards the end

of her life, a book that set out to imbricate science and theology in a meta-physical debate around climate and nuclear dystopia. Considering the formal and conceptual range of Hijab Imtiaz's work, it is shocking that Urdu scholarship never found readers or critics that would thoroughly re-examine the presuppositions of romanticism that have sedimented around her work. I believe that Sascha A. Akhtar has done precisely this with her translation of Hijab Imtiaz's *Adab-e-Zareen* as *Belles-Lettres*—not only has she introduced Hijab Imtiaz's work to a wider audience, but she has also re-introduced her work by infusing its romanticism with avant-garde modernism.

In the late 1930s and early 1940s, the free-verse experimentations of N.M. Rashid and Miraji broke away from earlier forms of Urdu poetry. Their work challenged the tradition of ghazals and other poetic forms that strictly adhered to certain requirements of rhyme, meter, and refrain. While the history of modernism in Urdu literature has countless twists and turns—from 19th-century supporters of colonial modernity to 20th-century anticolonial socialists—the formal experimentations of Rashid and Miraji pioneered a distinctly avant-garde direction that clearly separated itself from earlier modernists through its emphasis on free-verse poetry.

Hijab Imtiaz's themes generally tend towards the romantic, but her work also relies on formal experimentation that aligns it with the kind of avant-garde modernism that has come to be recognized by the work of Rashid and Miraji. In fact, before the publication of Rashid's debut collection, *Maavra* (1940), which is recognized as the first book of free-verse poetry in Urdu, this short book by Hijab Imtiaz, which barely gets a mention in the annals of Urdu literary history, was already busy undoing the binary between prose and poetry. Akhtar's translation is an important corrective in this regard. It forces us to reckon with Hijab Imtiaz's early experiments at the limit of genre, at the moment of prose and poetry's contamination. It also reminds us that reducing a woman writer whose work spans countless themes and forms to a romantic writer only exposes the narrowness of Urdu literary history and the absurdity of assuming that certain genders are naturally suited to certain genres.

Akhtar declares her subversive intent at the outset by choosing to translate *Adab-e-Zareen*, a short, forgotten text that has not garnered the same attention as the famous novels of Hijab Imtiaz. The book includes brief, reflective, and metaphysical texts about colours, weathers, internal and external landscapes, and imagination. The form of the texts—fluctuating between prose and poetry—is resolutely avant-garde. Hijab Imtiaz has labelled individual works within the book with different, sometimes wholly original,

genre categories. The categories, appearing as sub-headings, signal a playful tinkering with form: the sub-heading for the piece, 'The Advent of Evening', marks it as 'Verse Prose' (*Sher Mansour*); 'Song' is identified as a 'Prose Poem' (*Sher Mansour*); 'Flaxen Hair' is labelled—and this is my favourite—as 'a representational arrangement' (*Nazm numa nasr*).

Taking guidance from these experiments in the original book that blur the boundary between poetry and prose, Akhtar's translation emphasizes formal innovation by introducing elements that are not present in the original. For example, she introduces line breaks, shifting margins and indents, and white spaces. These poetic techniques disorient the continuous prose of the original. Akhtar captures this experimental spirit in the very title of the book, preferring to identify it as *Belles-Lettres*, an archaic genre that doesn't rely on the modern differences between self-sufficient categories like prose and poetry. It is both strange and exciting to see the ways in which Hijab Imtiaz's writings, usually dismissed as romances from a previous age, transform into pioneering works of the avant-garde that transgress the forbidding boundaries of genre in Akhtar's translation.

When I asked Akhtar why she chose to introduce these poetic techniques, she responded that she wanted to emphasize the pause. The pause—the poetic cut—is important to her because it stops the reader, makes them attend to the text, not pass over it in a rush to get to the next line. It shakes the sounds, colours, and other effects of the text, makes them unrecognizable, puts them out of beat, and before they resettle and recombine, the work of translation can happen.

The translation—in large part due to the emphasis on the pause—reads closely, haltingly, follows the sounds and forms of the text, and in this way, goes beyond the boundaries of romance to find other echoes. For example, where earlier translators have found 'singing' parrots, Akhtar finds 'screaming' parrots ['Missing Pages from the Book of Life']. By revealing images and rhythms that are only implicit in the original, by giving the original a new and different life, her translation unsettles both the meaning of the individual work and its place in literary history. Akhtar has successfully turned the act of translation into a creative act that opens new and supplementary meanings, new and supplementary genres, challenging the dictate to finalize and fix Hijab Imtiaz's writings.

Biographical Essay and Commentary

Rara Avis: Hijab Imtiaz Ali Taj and the Higher Realms of the Imagination

Dreaming is an odyssey whose destination is Truth. Before a person embarks on some great quest, they see a vision; they dream. This is why we cannot be dreaming all the time, nor be living and entirely happy in the reality outside of this. Both states are a requirement.

Hijab Imtiaz—Short Story Writer, Novelist, Pilot, and Denizen of the Imagination[1]

Some Context: Urdu Today

It is important to me as a translator to share my raison d'etre for this project. Hijab Imtiaz, her legacy, and her work are the inspiration, but I also have a wider socio-cultural concern which is to enrich Urdu literary scholarship.

'Nobody speaks Urdu anymore', says Alizay Jaffer, a young writer from Pakistan in an online forum. A statement such as this signifies death; death of a language, a heritage, and a superlative literary culture. The question that this statement begs to be asked is if nobody speaks Urdu anymore then are they only reading literature in English? We are focusing on Urdu but it is important to keep in mind that there are a staggering number of vernacular languages in the Subcontinent—close to 20,000.[2]

A few clarifications are necessary. Unfortunately, the Urdu language became attached to class, especially in the urban centres. Those with money have attended private schools where all the lessons are in English for decades. In fact, many have grown up almost completely oblivious to the fact that

---

[1] Video interview with Yousuf Kamran PTV Dast Go 1964.
[2] Article: *Matthias Weinreich*, 'Multilingualism in Pakistan', 2011. Soroso Programme.

Belles-Lettres. Sascha A. Akhtar, Oxford University Press. © Oxford University Press India 2022.
DOI: 10.1093/oso/9780190132644.003.0001

there is a strong Urdu-speaking, Urdu-reading, Urdu-writing intellectual community that has existed in the Subcontinent for centuries.

There are Urdu literary magazines, and always have been. There is poignant and stimulating discussion of literature in newspapers such as the Daily Jang in Pakistan, which was recently analysed by Dr Qamar Abbas[3] for its contribution towards literature, Nawaiwaqt, Anjaam, Imroz, and in more recent times literary journals Sawera, Dunyazad (which just ceased publication last year), Aaj. I discuss later the author Hijab Imtiaz's affiliation with Tahzīb-e Niswāñ/Women's Culture—the woman's literature magazine that ran for fifty years and Phool/Flower.

Yet generations have grown up entirely oblivious to this rich cultural underpinning of the literary history of the Subcontinent, which is essentially a history of a people.

The scope of this introduction does not allow me to delve into statistics, and I am certain that it is true that many, many people do not speak Urdu, or read Urdu or write in Urdu anymore. Apparently, even the NEET—a national entrance test for undergraduate studies in Medicine in India—recently dropped a provision allowing for the exam to be taken in Urdu.

However, I am also certain that this is simultaneously untrue. Through the reception to say, short story writer Aamer Hussein's evolution in fiction from writing in English, to writing in Urdu and the welcome he received, I am certain. Through the research I conducted for the purposes of this book and finding at the time of writing this, five academic articles just in 2018 published in the Urdu language about Hijab Imtiaz Ali Taj, I am certain. Through the excellent work of the website Rekhta (launched in 2013) dedicated to archiving Urdu literature, providing dictionaries and who have in 2018 launched a new tool called *Aamozish* for Urdu language learning.

In an article in *The Hindu* in 2017, writer Annie Zaidi blew the lid off of a whole new movement of *urdu-daans*.

A generation educated in English-medium schools couldn't even read the posters advertising the event. Besides, Urdu wasn't necessarily their scene. College fests had jazz and hip-hop rather than ghazals and qawwalis. The new leisure was gaming and memes, selfies and social media, Netflix and trying to chill. Couplets and metaphors?[4]

---

[3] Roznama Jang ki adabi khidmaat, it has just been published by Karachi University's Pakistan Study Centre.
[4] The New Urdu Cool. Annie Zaidi. GQ India, December 2017.

Describing a situation as discussed above she then goes on to throw a light on the trend reversal. She calls it the New Urdu.

> Stereotypes associated with Urdu, its ethos and its poets are, thankfully, dying out. You'd be hard pressed to spot a black sherwani in the mehfils and open mics where the most popular poets read. Today, Urdu wears jeans and T-shirts . . . when the new Urdu writes of its terror of death-by-nicotine, it ends up as a viral video.[5]

The resurgence is exciting. Much of it is social media driven, such as Manish Gupta's YouTube channel 'Hindi Kavita' which he followed up with Urdu Studio—allowing this 'new Urdu', to be accessible on a much wider scope than ever before. No boundaries exist, no partition. Those crusaders at the forefront of this work in India, such as Sanjiv Saraf (Founder of Rekhta), have no interest in the division. Saraf reiterates the fact that Urdu isn't 'just a language but a culture that transcends age, region and religion'.

Another figure who has made a stand for Urdu in this way is historian Rana Safvi, 'among those who reject the false binary of a Hindi/Urdu split along religious lines'. A pinned tweet on her own page says: "My name is Urdu and I am not a Muslim"'. She has established two Twitter handles @urdualfaz and @shairoftheday that have gone far to establish a new Urdu paradigm such as Annie Zaidi speaks of:

> The new Urdu doesn't take itself too seriously. Take Ishq Urdu, a Facebook page with around 2,55,000 followers. On August 15 this year, a still of Madhubala from the iconic 1960 film Mughal-e-Azam taking a selfie was posted, with the caption: Anarkali—Qile mein Ishq Urdu ki saalgirah par DJ party ke liye tayyar! (Anarkali is ready for the DJ party at the fort to celebrate Ishq Urdu's second birthday!).[6]

This fresh approach and attitude challenges notions of the 'purity' of Urdu and its traditions. 'More and more such a division between tradition and modernity does not hold in Urdu. I think it's a false binary to begin with. Urdu has been trying to "modernize" itself since the nineteenth century. People who stick to the "tradition" of Urdu are doing that tradition a big disservice.'[7]

---

[5] Ibid.
[6] Ibid.
[7] Translator interview with Professor, Writer, Translator, and Editor Haider Shahbaz, 2020.

It is into this environment that this translation of the work of a forgotten titan of Urdu Literature—an extraordinary prolific woman writer, Hijab Imtiaz enters.

It is a wonderful irony that our new generation of *urdu-daans* reference Anarkali in the above caption as it brings us naturally full circle, to the subject under discussion which is Hijab Imtiaz, whose life was entangled with the parents of the man who wrote Anarkali as well as with the man himself— Imtiaz Ali Taj.

The Early Years

Look how Nature has gifted a raison d'etre to everything she creates.

Raison D'Etre, p. 87

Hijab Imtiaz Ali nee Ismail, a woman whose life and works defied categorization or explanation was born in 1907 in Madras in District Arcot, which was part of the Carnatic Nawabdom (now Vaniyambadi).

By that time, the British had annexed the Carnatic Nawabdom, applying the doctrine of lapse. Azim Jah had been placed as the first Prince of Arcot, Amir-e-Arcot, in 1867 by Queen Victoria, and was given a tax free-pension in perpetuity.

It is unclear when she and her family re-located to Hyderabad, Deccan, but when talking about her early environment in interviews in her later years, she would cite Hyderabad as the place that really formed her. However, it is also clear that she would continually move between Madras and Hyderabad until she moved to Lahore, Punjab after her marriage.

My father loved two things, music and flowers. We had parties at our place in the evening and he would play the dil-ruba. He loved horticulture, there were flowers of every colour in our gardens. My mother loved reading and writing. In fact, her father's library was famous in Hyderabad Deccan ... so this is how I grew up ... flowers dancing in the breeze, books everywhere, the sounds of music.[8]

[8] Video interview with Yousuf Kamran; PTV Dast Go 1964—Transcribed and translated by Sascha Akhtar.

In a different interview whilst recalling her childhood, She talked of flowers, of kokilas, of riverbanks, the banks of the Godawari and Krishna, of mango-trees, and of the rainy season and was lost in a romantic haze.

'My father had a mango garden on the banks of the Krishna a few miles from Madras. I was in the habit of visiting this garden during the rainy season just for the sake of listening to the sweet shrill calls of the koel.'[9]

To Hijab, the early years of writers are the most formative. Often when asked about what appears to be a lifetime fascination with Nature and her perceived love of the Imaginary over 'Reality', she would talk of this.

'Three things influenced me as child—environment, surroundings and the state of affairs, and these are the things I write about to this day.'[10]

Hijab was an astute woman, a thinker, and without a doubt a classic polymath. Studies in psychology agree with the theory that our early years are the most important and Hijab was to in later years become well-versed in Psychology. She was a fan of the work of Sigmund Freud and studied him extensively—having developed a keen interest in the concept of the subconscious which was to develop into her Psychological Period of Literature, with works such as Andhera Khawab/Dream of Darkness1950, being representative of this period.

I myself, have known the magic and wonder of the sea since I was a child.

The Sea, p. 101

It is an understatement to describe the appearance of Nature in her work as a fascination. Nature is an actual character in all her work, and the current volume is no different. Landscape affects her characters implicitly and explicitly. Bird sounds, especially her beloved bulbul can change everything in one moment for a person in her stories. In Hijab's works, the Ocean provides powerful medicine to all who require it. This devotion to Nature is a large part of the Metaphysics of Hijab Imtiaz, especially as seen in Adab-E-Zareen, the volume being here introduced.

---

[9] Article on the occasion of her death by literary theorist, writer, and all-around culture vulture, Intezar Hussein (1925–2016) transcribed from older interviews.

[10] Video interview with Yousuf Kamran; PTV Dast Go 1964—Transcribed and translated by Sascha Akhtar.

Hijab Imtiaz nee Ismail's life can be charted as a symbolic timeline of major events in the history of the Subcontinent. Her life saw it all—the British Empire, the development of Literature, the Birth of Modernism, crucial natural disasters, the legacy of violence that was to ensue leading up to Partition. Having lived till 1999, she was a true witness to key times in the evolution of state and society and literary culture in the Subcontinent. She was active in writing a kind of account of the days of war in Lahore during the East Pakistan conflict in 1965. It was published as Mombatti ke Samne/By Candlelight. Blackout was observed at night and Hijab used to write this journal by candlelight.

In an interview in her later years she said:

> I feel that writers evolve with the times, and so too did I. In fact, I couldn't really help it etc. I kept writing and writing, and as I kept writing the style was the same, but the story changed. my view is that literature changes with the ages, and so I too changed with the ages. My characters however, stayed the same. I felt like they were family members. And it is also the case that those people are actually alive, at some time or the other. These were people who were with me in my childhood, and I continued to write about them throughout my life.[11]

Another speciality of Hijab's stories and novels was that she developed a mythology of characters that made re-appearances in different stories. Her famous characters Dr Gaar, Sir Harley, Dadi Zubeida, Habshan Zonash remained with her throughout her writing career which spanned over 60 years. Yet her readers were never bored. In fact, these characters formed a memorable part of the legend of Hijab Imtiaz Ali.

It is this kind of ability to change and keep changing that really sets Hijab's oeuvre apart. In a newly uncovered interview from the Lutfullah Archives, Hijab talks about how she began writing even before she could actually write, 'I would ask the older girls at school to write for me as I dictated to them'.[12]

That she was no ordinary young child, is further substantiated by the fact that she wrote her first novel Meri Natamaam Mohabbat at the age of 11. This novel was published and received by the literary world, launching her career. On the subject Hijab herself has expressed some disbelief at her own precocious nature, 'reflecting on this now I am quite shocked at myself having written such a story of desires and passions at such a young age[13]'.

---

[11] Audio interview with Hijab Imtiaz released 2018 from the Lutfullah Archives.
[12] Ibid.
[13] Ibid

In an article written in 2015, academic Haroon Ashraf has stated in The Nation that this very novel was considered, 'one of the greatest love stories ever written in Urdu Literature'.

Accolades such as this and more are Hijab's legacy. It may well be that she got pigeon-holed early on as the 'Queen of Romanticism', as she had a wide readership and was undoubtedly concerned with relationships, and the duelling of the sexes.[14]

Later in this essay, I make a case for Hijab Imtiaz as most certainly the Queen, but not of Romantics. She emerges for the 21st century, as the Queen of Metaphysics—a mystic. In reading the translation of Adab-E-Zareen, in which her majesty is resplendent, profound and truly from the realm of philosophy, spirituality and not just the love of a person for another but rather, Divine Love, the reader can decide whether this title is apt.

The constant rumination on worldly matters leads me astray from my true purpose.

Discord, p. 52

Apparently, by the mid-30s in the Subcontinent, lofty themes and romantic ideals were 'overtaken by the newly emerging trends of progressivism and modernism. The age of romanticism came to an end', which lent Hijab in the eyes of literary theorists and critics the onus of being the sole representative of 'the vanished age of romanticism, which had flourished in our literature during the '20s and early '30s'.[15]

What emerges from looking deeper into Hijab's life and works is that she was no last bastion of any one trope. Also, in the quote above, it seems the writer is describing the literary scenario in the West, in particular amongst male writers, when speaking of Modernism.

For the Subcontinent, there is no specific genre as 'romanticism', because our literary culture is steeped in ideas of love, and always has been. From the *ghazal* form to (mostly) the ideals of feminine beauty, courtship, and the essential union of the exclusively male and female in the culture; there is very little that does not emanate from themes of love from the perspective of the male gaze.

---

[14] Hijab Imtiaz Ali: The Queen of Romanticism, Haroon Ashraf, *The Nation* newspaper, 7 December 2015.
[15] Article on the occasion of her death by literary theorist, writer, and all-around culture vulture, Intezar Hussein (1925–2016) transcribed from older interviews.

The Hyderabad–Madras Years

During a global event that has come to be described as the so-called Third Plague Pandemic, the total number of Indians to die was greater than all other nationalities put together. By 1930, perhaps as many as 12 million people from the subcontinent had perished, mainly from just three provinces: Punjab, the United Provinces, and Bombay.[16] Whereas in much of the world the pandemic took the form of isolated flare-ups and outbreaks, in India it became endemic.

In the second year, epidemics were reported in Bengal, Madras, United Provinces, Central Provinces, Punjab, Mysore, Hyderabad, and Kashmir. It devastated almost the whole of India until about 1899. Up to the end of 1903, that deadly epidemic took the lives of about 2 million people according to state records, but the actual figures might be much more.

> I say to you this life which you and I believe so dear is a thing of chaos and fury. Is it not?.
>
> Conversation with A Girlfriend, p. 50, p. 33

The effect of this on young Hijab Ismail's life seems to have been considerable, for she was to talk of it throughout her lifetime. It appears that when she talks of the things that affect a writer, speaking from her own experience, the 'state of things', is one of four main things. In this regard, she believes that the fact that her father had to send her to Madras due to the plague left a deep impression on her.

Rudely uprooted from the idyllic childhood she has described in interviews, replete with music, books and beauty and in her writings, (especially in *Belles-Lettres*), it appears as if she was trying to preserve in some way those memories, and that place—a place that seems to have inspired her enough for a lifetime.

Hijab had a curiously Western Gothic sensibility which emerged as a pattern in all her works. This alone is a very unusual thing for literature of the Subcontinent by a woman, at the time she was writing in. In this regard, her title as 'Queen of the Romantics' seems to place her with the Victorian Romantics, however, on a critical examination of her work, it would appear

---

[16] Accounting for Plague in Colonial Indian Medicine; Nicholas H.A. Evans, *Medicine Anthropology Theory*, 25 June 2018.

she is closer to Emily Bronte and the Wuthering Heights high drama and High Gothic sensibility.

> I really cannot understand why the human race perceives this existence of ours as Nature's superior contrivance.
>
> Conversation with A Girlfriend, p. 56

Her entire oeuvre has dark and brooding overtones and literary critics at the time seemed to struggle with coming to terms with this, questioning her extensively about the deep dichotomies within her work between an almost ecstatic rendering of Nature and a deep brooding sense of foreboding.

In a paper written in 1958 by Begum Shaista Ikramullah Suhrawardy for the Journal of the Royal Society of Arts, she says:

> Hijab Imtiaz nee Ismail enjoyed great popularity but found no imitators; perhaps because her writing is so much an expression of her own strange personality, and therefore her works stands in isolation, neither bring influenced by the trends of her time, nor influencing others.

It appears Hijab was constantly asked questions about why she chose a realm of 'make-believe', over 'reality', a question which she would answer patiently with humility and elegance. One of her responses to a particularly aggressive interviewer (which we go into in-depth a little later), who was trying his best to level accusations of writing from a place of 'make-believe':

> I always find this very startling, as I write about life's truths that I learnt in childhood. I think it is all based on my childhood.[17]

It would make sense then that some of her sense of horror may have initially been inculcated when she went to Madras. In her own words she once described the south as a strange environment, 'strange like you wouldn't believe'.

In the interview with literary giant Intezar Hussain, she described:

> The days I lived in Madras were beautiful. But the nights were terrifying. Very close to our house was a burning ghat. It was quite horrifying to see a dead body being burnt to ashes.

---

[17] Audio interview with Hijab Imtiaz released 2018 from the Lutfullah Archives.

From the age of 6 to 13, Hijab, her sister Zakiya Bibi and her mother and possibly other women in the extended family were to live in Madras. There may have been passage between the two centres of Hyderabad and Madras. Her early education took place at home under the tutelage of her father. Later she studied English at the missionary school. Her mother was a student of Urdu and so along with English, she also had Urdu lessons. Her father, Syed Mohammad Ismail was the first secretary to the Nizam of Hyderabad and her mother Abbasi Begum was one of the very few women active at the time as a scholar and writer.

It is clear from this that in the family she was born into, there was no question of women remaining uneducated or treated as second- or even third-class citizens, as most assuredly could well have been the case in other families at the time, with other young women she knew, her peers and her friends. In this regard, the darker aspects of patriarchy, such as suppression of education or independence, did not fall on Hijab. This is important to know, because hers was not a common-place experience for women of the time and helps in understanding her work.

It explains her meritorious rise for one, unimpeded and encouraged by her mother and father, there was nothing to stop her. In a newly released audio interview from the Lutfullah Archive, she describes her desire to write as a child as insatiable.

'I could not sleep unless I wrote my stories. I had no choice,' she has described. These things are telling of advanced intellect, that unimpeded by socio-cultural impediments was allowed to run with it and go as far as possible, even to the skies as she was to do later.

Even though the requirement to leave Hyderabad and go to Madras seemed problematic to her, in Madras, Hijab began her grand love affair with the ocean. The Ocean features centrally in her works and most markedly in *Belles-Lettres*. Also, descriptions of heat and sub-tropical climes make their appearance, however, Hijab was always to identify with Hyderabad as her birth right.

When asked in this same interview about the question of writing in Urdu, Hijab becomes impassioned about her heritage and being from the centre of Urdu itself—Hyderabad, Deccan; a place where the arts and literature and music flourished.

This is an important thing to bear in mind when considering Hijab's language. In his translator's introduction writer and translator, Aamer Hussein has described the language of *Belles-Lettres* as '(employing) a linguistic register that combines a classical, Arabic- and Persian-inflected lexicon with a

syntax of colloquial intimacy and startling lucidity'.[18] It is this classical lexicon that Hyderabad has always been synonymous with as a centre of culture
and art.

> Perhaps this is yearning. Everything large or small under the sun reminds
> me of your grandeur.

Yearning, p. 59

There are few cities in the world that can claim to be founded by a poet, and
Hyderabad holds this distinction. Muhammad Quli Qutb Shah (1565–11
January 1612) was the fifth sultan of the Qutb Shahi dynasty of Golkonda
who founded the city of Hyderabad. He was an accomplished poet and wrote
his poetry in Persian, Telugu, and Urdu. He is accepted as the first author in
the Urdu language composing his verses in the Persian diwan style, and his
poems consisted of verses relating to a single topic, gazal-i musalsal.

After printing was introduced in Hyderabad the literary spectrum expanded exponentially. In 1824, the first collection of Urdu *Ghazals* named
Gulzar-e-Mahlaqa (Mahlaqa's garden of flowers) written by Mah Laqa Bai,
was printed and published from Hyderabad.

After the Revolt of 1857, many Urdu writers, scholars, and poets who
lost their patronage at Delhi made Hyderabad their home, that grew and
brought reforms in the literary and poetry work. Scholars continued to mi-
grate to Hyderabad during the reign of Asaf Jah VI and his successor Asaf
Jah VII. These included Shibli Nomani, Dagh Dehlvi, Fani Badayuni, Josh
Malihabadi, Ali Haider Tabatabai, Zahir Dehlvi, and many others.

The reign of Asaf Jah VII saw many reforms in literary work. For the first
time in history the Nizams introduced Urdu as a language of court, admin-
istration, and education. Other notable poets, scholars, and writers of the
early 20th century are Amjad Hyderabadi, Maharaja Sir Kishen Pershad,
Makhdoom Mohiuddin, Sayyid Shamsullah Qadri, Mohiuddin Qadri Zore,
and Sulaiman Areeb.

It is almost certain that Hijab had known of, read, and most likely met
many of these poets and writers. It is also almost certain that her father and
mother knew almost everyone in the literary world residing in Hyderabad.
The parties held regularly that Hijab talked of fondly must have seen many a
writer, many a chat in the gardens with the young Hijab.

---

[18] Asymptote Journal 2011 tr. Aamer Hussein.

It is no surprise then that she wrote her first book at the age of 11 and a half. She may have been incredulous of this later in life, but upon examining her early years and in her own words, 'the environment, the atmosphere and the state of things', it makes complete sense.

Hijab's mother would have been a formidable and inspiring person to have as a parent. Abbasi Begum's status as an Urdu scholar and writer also makes complete sense in the environment of Hyderabad, with *her* own father's library being prominent amongst the many repositories present at the time such as the Asifia Kutubkhana established in 1891 (now known as the State Central Library of Hyderabad) which is the biggest library of Telangana.

It appears Abbasi Begum was a dedicated and prolific writer, as Hijab talked of this in an interview later in life. Certainly, she was one of the very few female writers at the time, which is in itself extraordinary. Atiya Faizee, Mohammadi Begum, Jenahara Begum, and Valida Afzal Ali were some of her contemporaries.

The literary journal Tahzīb-e Niswāñ was a game-changer for women writers, from 1898 when it made its appearance as a literary journal for women in Lahore and Abbasi Begum's work was known because of it. It would continue to be important during Hijab's later literary career also, and synchronistically was founded by the parents of Imtiaz Ali Taj, who 'insisted to Sir Syed Khan that a journal for women was necessary, even though Sir Syed did not agree'.[19] Abbasi Begum in fact and Imtiaz Ali Taj's mother were friends, long before there was any notion of Hijab and Taj becoming betrothed.

> I stand silently for many hours at my window overlooking the garden, listening to the cheerless notes of some lovelorn bird.
> The Advent of Afternoon, p. 110

About her mother, Hijab has said, 'Her concerns were the same as women writers such as Atiya Faizee and those are the things she talked to me about. As a child, I always saw her writing'.[20]

Atiya Faizee was one of the first elite Indian Muslim women to receive a modern education, appear in public unveiled, and participate in women's organizations. She was a writer, an iconoclast in many ways, another example of

---

[19] Translator interview with Yasmine and Naeem Tahir in their home. Lahore, 2019.
[20] Audio interview with Hijab Imtiaz released 2018 from the Lutfullah Archives.

one of these highly intellectual, learned, fearless women of the Subcontinent of the time. She married a painter named Samuel Rahamin who changed his faith from Judaism to Islam upon marrying her. Her creative force knew no bounds, from classical Indian music to choreography.

The reason this is important is because if what Hijab says is true about early influences and the environment being crucial in a writer's development, then indeed Atiya Faizee may well have been an influence on the young Hijab. She too would marry a fellow creative and become part of a 'power couple'. She too would be instrumental in the promotion and progression of literary culture by hosting salons and connecting other creatives.

Hijab's marriage later to a fellow *wunderkind*, Imtiaz Ali Taj, who had risen meritoriously to fame with the publication of the immortal story *Anarkali*, was much feted and celebrated. The union is even memorialized in fiction by the celebrated female writer Quratul-Ain-Hyder (1927–2007).

In almost every interview, Hijab tirelessly and always elegant and humble answers the questions of obviously fascinated (and sometimes overzealous) journalists about how she and her beau (when talking about him in interviews she would always call him Taj *sahib*) got together, how they lived together as writers and whether there were clashes and so forth.

It is clear from historical material, that they were both prodigies. Hijab, with her novel at 11 and a half, and Taj with his arrival on the dramatic scene at twenty something.

Hijab and Taj

It was said about Hijab Ismail that theirs was a match made as a literary alliance. In an interview, Hijab herself remarked on this in an interview, 'It may well be true that it was a beneficial literary alliance, but above all it was a romance and a successful one'.

Syed Imtiaz Ali Taj was born in 1900 in Lahore. His father Syed Mumtaz Ali was a high-ranking scholar who did a great deal for the cause of Urdu. It was he, who founded Tahzīb-e Niswāñ in 1898. Imtiaz Ali Taj himself was to create a children's magazine Phool. At the time, these magazines were very popular with both women and children and published essays by well-known writers.

We have established that Hijab wrote from an early age. Whilst her own mother was active as a writer, being published in Tahzīb-e Niswāñ—Imtiaz Ali Taj's mother was the editor of the magazine. They were all based in Lahore,

and Hijab and her family were based in South India, so they were separated by great physical distance. When Taj's mother passed away, he became editor and it was Hijab who was contributing stories.

'In this way, we had old, established and continuous dealings with the family,' said Hijab in one of her interviews. She and Taj began corresponding, which was the beginning of their relationship.

It is clear from things Hijab has narrated in various interviews that those letters were the beginning of their courtship. Much later, regarding this time and the letters, Hijab was to disclose,

'All those beautiful memories are still in my mind. It makes me happy to think of that time. Together, via the medium of letters, we inhabited a world of our own creation'[21].

Taj did visit Madras eventually, and Hijab describes it in her own words simply as, 'he saw me and I saw him', perhaps to subtly intimate that it was love at first sight. 'We had already become close through our correspondence, so it was a natural progression.'[22]

Apparently, during the days of courtship, Hijab and Taj would fight. Six months before their marriage they had a terrible fight which Hijab herself confessed nearly split them asunder.

What is the purpose of the frenetic motion of life? You say you are able to live in the darkness of night without a guiding light but what is the purpose of that life?

Love of Another, p. 58

If we try to establish a timeline for the narrative from the interviews and material we have at hand, it can be deduced that their courtship began when Hijab was quite young. This fight that they had that nearly ruined them was resolved when the 20-year-old playwright made a grand gesture. His groundbreaking play *Anarkali* was to be dedicated to the young Hijab.

She has said that had he not done this—they would probably not be together. *Anarkali* was written in 1922, when Hijab was 15. However, their marriage year is 8 years later in 1930. Therefore, the fight could not have been

---

[21] Lutfullah Archives; Interview 2 released 2019.
[22] Ibid.

six months before their marriage as Hijab spoke of in her interview in around 1964 on the show *Dastan Go* hosted by Yousuf Kamran.

Hijab re-located to Lahore with Taj upon being married in 1930 in Bulhari. She pursued her writing without cessation and also took on editorial duties in connection with the two family journals—*Tehzeeb-I-Niswan* and *Phool*.

Imtiaz Ali Taj really was at the centre of Lahore literary life, spearheading activity and embodying the very spirit of it. He was later to be lauded as one of the greatest Urdu dramatists who ever lived.

He was also a great repository of memories of the early days of Radio Lahore. Hijab was witness to all this. Conversations with her in later life were invaluable for the collective wealth of knowledge of two fascinating figures of Urdu Literature.

Hijab was to say that luckily, because Taj was in drama and she wrote short stories, they had no literary disagreements. 'Perhaps if I had written drama or he short stories, there would have been more of a conflict of interests, but as it stood, thankfully we did not have issues with each other.'[23]

It seems the time they had together, was full and vibrant. In her 1964 interview Hijab talks of the great literary friends of Imtiaz Ali Taj, such as Hasrat, Shaukat Thanavi, Patras Bukhari, and his wife who frequented their house day and night. She describes their debates that would go on and on endlessly. They were sweet arguments. Arguments with a purpose. There was always a horizon to be reached. It was not just fighting without any rhyme or reason.[24]

As Imtiaz Ali Taj was on the film censor board for 13 years—films were shot at their house. Hijab Imtiaz acted as match-maker during one of these shoots. 'The lead actor was Shaukat Hussain Rizvi. Our bungalow was being used as the location for this film. Noor Jehan (the Queen of song herself) was 16 years old at the time and it was during the filming that she and Shaukat fell in love. They went off to Mumbai to be married. Noor Jehan still comes to visit me.'[25]

For those fascinated by the literary alliance of Hijab Ismail and Imtiaz Ali Taj—the fact is that it didn't in the cold light of reality last very long after their marriage.

---

[23] Video interview with Yousuf Kamran; PTV Dast Go 1964—Transcribed and translated by Sascha Akhtar.
[24] Ibid
[25] Ibid.

The Murder of Taj

We are fortunate that for the purposes of documentation, we have a primary source for how the story was to come to an end in the form of a newly released video from the Lutfullah Archive.

In this interview, the writer herself narrated the events that led up to a fateful night in 1970—40 years after their marriage. I will here endeavour to share parts of the transcript as a first-hand account, for I do not believe anyone else to be a more reliable narrator. This is how the story Hijab tells begins:

'Imtiaz had a step-brother—Hameed Ali, whom he cared for very much. He doted on his nieces and nephews as well, but every so often, I would get the impression that Hameed Ali harboured jealousy for Imtiaz.

I mentioned this to him, but he took offence at the thought, saying only, "He cannot be jealous. He is my dear brother." Hameed Ali would not even lay eyes on Imtiaz's face, but Imtiaz continued to try to go to him, even though he and his side of the family never met with us. They never gave us the time of day!

The properties of the families were combined and when the matter of distributing property arose, according to Begum Hijab, Hameed Ali refused to give us any portion saying, 'You only have one daughter, and I have two sons'.

Hijab did not speak of religion much as she did not believe that writers were under any obligation to participate in religiopolitical debate or religiopolitical opinion. When narrating the story of the two brothers, however, she disclosed her family's affiliations: We are People of Tashi'a. According to our beliefs, girls get exactly the same as the boys do. Which is why I would say to him, 'Our daughter has just as much a right as your sons,' but Hameed Ali repeatedly dismissed this.

Warring and violence over matters of property is a well-worn subcontinental socio-cultural trope. The series of events that followed in the case of Imtiaz Ali Taj echo those narratives. The elders of the family and other relations advised Imtiaz to take the matter to court, but Hijab reports that he said, 'I can't stand against my brother in court!' The matter did end up in court but the outcome as property battles historically go did not come till much later. One night, Imtiaz was working till around 1 am on his magazine, *Phool*. Having completed his work, he came to bed. Summer was upon us. We would sleep on the veranda at the top of the house. On this night at around 2 am,

two unknown men attacked Imtiaz. I was asleep on the *charpai* next to him. The attackers wounded him 9 times. He was bathed in blood. I was wounded right near my heart. I have the scar to this day.[26]

The next day at noon, Imtiaz Ali Taj unable to fight for his life anymore, died from his wounds. This was in 1970. The police thought he was murdered over the inheritance. The murderers were arrested but later released, suspected Hijab says in her interview to have been bribed.

The strange irony to the story is that before Imtiaz was murdered, his brother Hameed too died from an incurable illness. 'And I recall, even then Imtiaz would go to take care of him,' says Hijab.

A tragedy had befallen Hijab and her only daughter, Yasmine. According to one writer she 'became an observer rather than a participant in society', for a while.

'I am very affected by Taaj Sahib, I always have been and always will be. This is because he was so naturally decent, and a strange chap because he never interfered in anyone's business. Many people have said many things about him, but what I will say is that there are few people born like Imtiaz Ali Taj,' she said in an interview in her later life.[27]

Yasmine Tahir, Hijab Imtiaz, and Taj's only child says to this day she wonders how her mother actually lived through the years to come following the violent and disturbing events of her husband's death. 'Mummy was such a sensitive person, even 20 years after her death, I still wonder how she found the strength to carry on.' [28]

The truth is that Yasmine and Hijab had a loyal ally in the form of Yasmine's husband Naeem Tahir, who was not only a family member but a mentee of Imtiaz Ali Taj, whom he had looked up to and had dealings with before meeting Yasmine.

It is clear from conversations with Naeem Tahir, that Taj's death had a deep impact on him. He has been a relentless archivist of Imtiaz Ali Taj and Hijab Imtiaz's works, and a passionate researcher. He narrates a story of a rare film made by a German filmmaker, *Loves of a Mughal Prince* in which Imtiaz Ali Taj, along with his buddies R. Peerzada and Patras Bukhari appeared, that he has been tracking for decades only to get a lead on it in 2018. The film itself is not in his hands yet, 'but I have seen the stills', he shares with a degree of satisfaction. In this film, Imtiaz Ali Taj plays Akbar himself.

---

26 Lutfullah Archives; Interview 2 released 2019.
27 Audio interview with Hijab Imtiaz released 2018 from the Lutfullah Archives.
28 Translator's interview with Yasmine and Naeem Tahir in their home; Lahore 2019.

In the room that Hijab spent her last decade, a glass-fronted cupboard stands that belonged to Taj. 'This cupboard is over 100 years old,' shares Naeem Tahir. The shelves are filled with the most special books he has collected, some are wrapped in plastic. Next to the one cupboard is one that looks identical. It is a replica Naeem has had made.

In narrating the death of Taj, tears come to everyone's eyes, and the emotion is palpable. Naeem and Yasmine have a diwan in one of their lounges. It has been re-upholstered, but it was the last place Imtiaz Ali Taj sat after his vicious attack, as he lay bleeding. Hijab as we know sustained an injury, but this was not accidental. 'She was so courageous, she actually tried to stop Daddy's attackers,' Yasmine Tahir tells us.

Naeem Tahir was working in Islamabad at the time of the death with the PNCA. 'They would not allow me to travel to Lahore to help my family, so I quit. Hijab and Yasmine needed me.' To Hijab and Taj, Naeem was not merely an outsider who had become part of the family, rather 'it was as if he had always been part of our family and just melded in seamlessly'. Later Hijab was to say 'Naeem is like that large tree that gives shade to all under whose protection Yasmine and I have sat', shares her daughter Yasmine. She shares that this is a quote from her mother that has stayed with her throughout her life.

Naeem was also the one who would not rest until they found out exactly who murdered Imtiaz Ali Taj and why. A special team, set up by the President of Pakistan at the time, was assigned to the job. After much analysis and discovery it was clear that it was not Imtiaz Ali Taj's family but a hired hitman. Taj was to be a key witness in a case that would uncover a large crime ring. The Majlis Tariqi Adab/Board for Advancement of Literature did not realize how far forward Taj had put himself in harm's way in order to get justice for them. The criminals had embezzled and defrauded the organization.

Rara Avis

Hijab . . . was an other-worldly creature. The way she lived her life and the manner in which she spoke were like the worlds in her stories. She was in fact a character from her stories.
—Asma Irum; Urdu Council Oct 2017

The inimitable storyteller, Hijab Imtiaz was from all accounts, not just one thing. Neither just a woman, or a woman writer, or a writer, or a wife, she

was many things all at once, people have, as the journalist above—called her *otherworldly, strange, unusual* because she was in fact like a character of the imagination.

She was a *rara avis*. A term from the Latin found in the Juvenales satires (6.165) from the 2nd century A.D. *Rara avis in terris nigroque simillima cycno* ('a bird as rare upon the earth as a black swan').

From all that is known of Hijab, I am quite certain that if she knew of this phrase, which she may well have done—she would be amused knowing it had been applied to her.

She narrates a story in an interview about how she was sitting in her garden writing (which is a continuous theme in *Belles-Lettres*), when she observed an eagle fly down and land. The manner in which its claws functioned to facilitate the landing fascinated her. 'I thought it would be a great to learn to fly myself.'

This then would prove to be the moment that Hijab Imtiaz would decide to challenge herself by learning to fly a plane. 'She wanted to be beyond the bounds of the earth', says Naeem Tahir, her beloved son-in-law, 'so she flew above it!' It is not clear how long it took her to get to the point where she joined the Lahore Flying Club, from the time she decided this, but her license was obtained in October 1936.

It is important to contextualize this to some extent. In 1920, the airplane was only 17 years old—a modern wonder that most people witnessed from the side-lines in theatre newsreels and barnstorming air shows.

By the end of the decade, however, the airplane had become a phenomenon that one could experience first-hand. Brave souls could travel by passenger airline service or compete to set a flight record like Charles Lindbergh and Amelia Earhart.

The airplane had moved front and centre in the imagination. Just as it did in Hijab's imagination from her observation of the eagle to actually taking to the skies. She was very much 'of the time'—but a rarity in the Subcontinent, seeing as she was to take the title of first female pilot.

There is a famous passage from Ernest Hemingway:

Then the plane began to move along the ground, bumping like a motorcycle, and then slowly rose into the air. We headed almost straight east of Paris, rising in the air as though we were sitting inside a boat that was being lifted by some giant, and the ground began to flatten out beneath us.

It looked cut into brown squares, yellow squares, green squares and big flat blotches of green where there was a forest. I began to understand cubist painting.

—Ernest Hemingway in The Toronto Daily Star, 9 September 1921

It has been said that Aviation birthed Modernism. It offered artists a compelling image for interpreting modernity. In America artists 'developed an aesthetics of their own, based on the machine'.[29]

The most exemplified phase of Western Modernism referred to as 'High Modernism', occurred during the inter-war years (1918–1939). This was the time when writers synonymous with Modernism, such as Virginia Woolf, James Joyce, T.S. Eliot, and D.H. Lawrence, thrived.

While Victorians typically concerned themselves with rendering reality as they understood it into fiction, novels like *Tristram Shandy* (1759), which lacks a clear plot and in which the protagonist narrates his own birth—and *Jude the Obscure* (1895)—a bleak novel that savagely critiqued Victorian customs can be seen as forerunners to a period that extolled the divergent and experimental. In the West, that is.

Hijab seems to have in her own way symbolized the Modernist *zeitgeist* birthing her *own* movement in the Eastern literary tradition. She often talked about how writers should evolve with the times, in fact, she said, 'I sometimes feel as if there was no other way for me but to evolve'.

In the Journal of the Royal Society of the Arts,[30] Begum Shaista Suhrawardy Ikramullah, Pakistani author, politician, diplomat, and social-activist whose life bridges the late colonial and post-colonial phases of South Asian history has described with great clarity the position Hijab held in the literary history of the Subcontinent, 'her attitude and style are totally different from those of her contemporaries . . . She is an escapist *par excellence* . . . She takes the reader into a dream-world, into an atmosphere of "might and light and half-light" . . . and perhaps the great popularity (of her works) in the 30's is due to the fact that they presented such a complete contrast to the works of other writers of that time'.

I do not associate myself with any literary circles.

Hijab Imtiaz, Lutfullah Archives

It is not, however, that simple. As discussed earlier, she has been called a heavy romantic and was known for her 'romances'. She called herself 'a Victorian'. From the range and depth of her work, it is clear that her work transcends all these things.

---

[29] Brooklyn Museum material for exhibition on Machine Age art, 17 October 1986 through 16 February 1987.
[30] *Journal of the Royal Society of Arts*, Vol. 106, No. 5025, August 1958.

At times, symbolist, at times Gothic Romantic—where despair, pining, and wretchedness are prevalent. In the same article cited above, Suhrawardy remarks, 'It is difficult to decide in which country the scene is laid, for the setting has all the voluptuous richness, romance and colour that one associates with oriental harems, together with the luxurious modernity of a Fifth Avenue flat'.

So there was a certain kind of opulence to her work which had more in common with *Fin de Siècle* Western works, more than anything else, especially its 'literary and artistic climate of sophistication, world-weariness, and fashionable despair'.[31]

Fin de Siècle has also been called 'an umbrella term embracing symbolism'. There was also 'the swirling, sometimes abstracted, aerial imagery of Futurism's final incarnation, *aeropittura* (painting inspired by flight), arrived by the 1930s emerged from the Futurists' interest in modern aircraft and photographic technologies'.[32]

There had been no other female pilots on the Subcontinent. It does not seem that this was something that even occurred to Hijab. As she said, it was a *moment of inspiration.*

She was then to join the now, Lahore Flying Club founded in her era by a group of dedicated philanthropists initially named as 'Northern India Flying Club'.

This is the first flying club established in Indo-Pak Sub Continent in 1932. The future of the club was tenuous at the time of partition were not for the dedication of a few individuals. 'When I joined Lahore's Northern India Flying Club there were 300 members, but the actual flying members were just about 10 or 15 and I was the first female member,' Hijab narrates in an interview very matter-of-factly.

From the interview the viewer can tell that it simply was never an issue for her whether she was a woman, or whether there were other women there. She was clear on the matter and so in October 1936, Hijab received her pilot's license, again achieving things in the manner of a maverick.

The following translation from the transcript of an interview with journalist is worth quoting in full:

---

[31] Encyclopaedia Brittanica entry on Fin de siècle ART.
[32] Guggenheim material for *Italian Futurism: Reconstructing The Universe* 21 February–1 September 2014.

I got my A license that is accepted internationally. When I joined the club people were surprised. Many men were even jealous. Usually you get a certificate in 40 hours, over a number of months, but I somehow past all my flying lessons in 21 hours! And when I went up in the air alone, my heart was beating very fast, but I remembered God and managed to make a successful landing. And everyone congratulated me even the ones who were jealous and were glad I had gotten my license.[33]

And so the *rara avis* was born. One whose work thrilled readers for decades to come.

A poem penned by poet Adeeb Malegalvi marking the occasion was published in *Tehzeeb-I-Niswan* in the same year, 1936.

It is here presented in translation for the first time:

Has Hijab's fearlessness unveiled the secret,
that even caged prisoners have the will to fly.
For those deep in disbelief for centuries,
this event is a miracle for this nation.

She was solely confined to the four walls
Now she has broken barriers and soared in the restful skies

Why shouldn't your taking to the skies be a good omen?
This door of progress that you have opened is a step for all

Those labouring under outmoded beliefs are in disbelief
At the incongruence of woman meant to submit in an aeroplane—

Your victory is due a thousand praises
It has effaced, far and wide the fear of the Unknown—
Translated by Rukhsar Amir & Sascha Akhtar

Flying was to be Hijab's passion, besides reading and writing. She frequently participated in Lahore flying club's competitions. Shafiq-ur-Rahman,[34] the distinguished author, shared an anecdote regarding Hijab in his biography.

---

[33] Video interview 1 Lutfullah Archives; Released 2018. Transcribed and translated by Sascha Akhtar.

[34] Translator's interview with Yasmine and Naeem Tahir in their home; Lahore 2019.

He stated that he visited Hijab's house and was sitting in her lawn when she came to greet him. Hijab told him that she had to go somewhere and would come back in a short while. A little time had elapsed when he saw a small plane circling above the lawn where he was sitting. Lifting up his head, he was surprised to see that it was Hijab in the plane above, waving her handkerchief towards him.

Hijab took her flying further than leisure, Naeem Tahir shares, 'one thing I know for sure in this regard is that she flew during World War II, delivering army mail'.

As a far as French Literature goes, we are aware from Aamer Hussein's Translator's Introduction in *Asymptote* (2011), that she was familiar with and possibly enjoyed the work of Symbolist poet Pierre Louys.

If we take Hijab's own words on the matter, 'I love to read on any and every subject and I feel that unless we read, we cannot write'. Eventually she even wrote a science-based novel.

'I feel a writer cannot be a true writer unless they read up on their subject. You need extensive knowledge to write. So my knowledge grew a little after reading up, so I wrote a science-based novel on radiation and the atom and nuclear bombs called *Pagal Khana*. I had to read a lot of science even though it was not my subject but then I got very fascinated/interested and started enjoying them as if I was some kind of expert'. This kind of level of attention to detail further belies a very keen intellect which she exhibited from an early age.

In these later romances Hijab has recourse to a rather macabre type of adventure story; they are written in imitation of the early English and American stories of blood and slaughter, but she somehow succeeds in imparting her brand of romantic aura to these as well. Strange islands, ruins, and haunted castles on the outskirts of African and American deserts are chosen as scenes for eerie stories of murder, poisoning, and intrigue. The plots are well constructed, the endings always unexpected, and in most cases, it turns out that the strange occurrences that gave rise to such fears are traced to some quite harmless cause. Begum Suhrawardy believed that because Hijab's work was so singular, 'The short story continued to concern itself with social and political problems which were further accentuated by partition and the debacle that followed after it.'

Raison d'etre

It is clear from what we have looked at above that a *rara avis*, such as Hijab was, transcends definition, but it is very helpful to contextualize certain aspects of her life and works in order to reach some kind of clearer understanding of her place in Urdu Literature.

Adab-e-Zareen or *Belles-Lettres* was a very rare little collection that managed to see light of day in between the monolithic tomes this prolific and prodigious writer put out. Amidst all the fanfare over her as a novelist—this resplendent, gleaming MS may have never seen light of day, etc.

Her concerns are the concerns of the early 20th-century French philosophers. In this way *Belles-Lettres* is no ordinary fiction but a philosophical tract on Metaphysical issues. There is also a very strong Buddhist-like dialogue on matters of impermanence and duality. Having visited Begum Hijab's home and spoken to her family and seen the titles in her private libraries— situating her in a wider scope of literature and thought is a legitimate stance.

Transcripts from interviews conducted by Intezar Hussein depict her *raison d'etre* well:

'The blue sky fascinated me very much. I developed a craze for flying high in the sky. That led me to try to become a pilot.' And she added: 'The blue sky and twinkling stars overhead, and down on earth the rice fields, flowers, birds, cats—these are the things that fascinate me. I like to depict them in my novels.

Hussein ventures to interrupt her: 'This may well prompt a progressive to brand you as an escapist.' 'This is not escapism,' she replied, 'and this is not art for art's sake. I believe in art for life's sake. A starry sky is very much a part of our life, or is it not?'

Her art was very much about being in the moment. In fact, as the reader will find in the translations in the second half of this volume +, the moment is excavated and re-created in such infinitesimal detail at times, it is as if witnessing a Dutch representational painting from the 1600s. Later on in this essay, we will learn about her naming of certain pieces such as the prose Flaxen Hair (p. 106), which she calls a 'representational arrangement'.

That is what the experience is like—very present. Again, it is because of the *singular* nature of her work that looking further afield beyond her immediate literary psychogeography and even to other art forms create a kind of resonance.

Stars coruscate with aplomb in the sky on a hot night.

Even the most insignificant bit of cloud can obscure their light, rendering the star-beams invisible on earth—yet their innate nature to shine does not suffer in the slightest. They remain unchanged; a perpetual dance of light.

Treatise against Eternal Death Inspired by a Shadow, p. 69

Hijab said she did not believe in art for art's sake as mentioned above, however, similar to the French Symbolists, she did have this deep-rooted belief that art must exist for its *own* sake. Hijab said categorically that she never wrote for an audience. She wrote above all for herself, and 'if someone likes what I write then I am fortunate, but by the same token if they do not, I am not affected by this'.

She also eschewed ideological or religio-political comment in fiction. She did not wish for her fiction to be 'reformative':

'On one occasion', shares Intezar Hussein, while talking about the Islamic system as presented by maulvis and mullahs, she told me: 'I, too, have done a lot of thinking on this question. I had also prepared an outline of an Islamic system as I understood it and had sent it to Z.A. Bhutto when he was in power'.

'But', I interjected, 'your fiction doesn't provide a clue to your involvement in questions of this nature'.

She wondered at my remark and said: 'Why should it provide such a clue? This has nothing to do with my fiction'.[35]

Symptomatic of the duality of the life, work, and nature of Hijab Imtiaz, she would also throughout her life need to defend her work. She maintained that her characters were very much crafted 'from real life'.

It seems, in trying to come to terms with the rich and nuanced works of literature that Hijab Imtiaz gave her readership, critics at the time hoisted multiple theories and levelled varying criticisms on her, the point always being a variation of the theme, that her work 'did not ring true of the times', or that she was a 'fantasist'.

In one interview she talks about being asked why she didn't write about rural life, to which she coolly replied, 'I have never lived in a rural area. I have no knowledge or experience of this. A writer should only write about what they know'.

---

[35] Article on the occasion of her death by literary theorist, writer, and all-around culture vulture, Intezar Hussein (1925–2016) transcribed from older interviews.

Yousuf Kamran's interview referenced several times in this essay on his show *Dastan Go* in 1964 may well be taken as an indication, of the manner in which her work was perceived.

As the interview has never before been transcribed and translated into English, it seems apropos to include a part of it in full here, as it illustrates precisely the kind of nuanced literary discourse that Hijab's work was a part of, but perhaps also what she as the *rara avis* that she was had to encounter:

Yousuf Kamran (henceforth referenced as 'Interviewer'): 'We find realism in our short stories vs subjective reality. The short story writers of the time write in the area of realism and our writers would use the novel form for the world of imagination. If you look at the onset of Urdu literature, it is very much realism based . . . but the realism we find in your work is very much a subjective reality. Is it that you are more interested in the hidden rather than the apparent?

Hijab Imtiaz: It is not that I am an introvert. Is that what you're talking about? i.e the phenomenon of the introvert vs extrovert?

Interviewer: Yes in a way. I mean is it not a form of self-conceitedness that a writer uses the lens of themselves for everything?

Hijab Imtiaz (After some thought and with her trademark elegance): Yes I think you're right, but many artists despite using themselves as a lens for their work and sitting alone and creating their work re-enter society *via* their art. The result of the solitude and self-reflection is to enter society via their art . . . and ultimately what is the difference between one's life and art?

Interviewer: Well, yes but I was referring to say the world of ideas . . . or the realm of thought . . . so the imaginary can become reality in many stories . . . but to us living in the real world they do in fact appearing belonging to the realm of make-believe, magic and mystery. However they come to us.

Hijab Imtiaz: Well, I actually feel they were visionary coming to is in stories that have now become realities.

Interviewer: Ok well will you agree with me on one point that that today's symbolic stories have transformed the realm of thought in that they have taken the abstraction of the stories and applied it to today's world, so creating new interpretations.

Hijab Imtiaz: In today's writing the desires of people are not depicted as much as mundane worries. It is all smoke and mirrors. People were interested in magic, and fairies today, stories instead of showing us the writers desires and dreams use smoke and mirrors with words to fool people.

Interviewer: Are you talking about the art of story with plot and of course structures in place, beginning, middle and end vs the 'anti-novel' or 'anti-story' movement that has been going on? Are you saying it does harm to the status of the short story?

Hijab Imtiaz: No I don't say that but there is a kind of dishonesty. I want to ask those writers if I get a chance. What is the point?

Interviewer: I would argue that the inner workings of the mind that has no plot, no continuity, say stream of consciousness if that is narrated is that not closer to true reality, if you put it down, without editing it, to give to a reader as art—in a pure form.

Hijab Imtiaz: If that is aim of the writer then that is a grand enterprise. But I have read a few symbolic short stories where I felt the reader would feel quite lost and couldn't follow.

Interviewer: I wonder if you make the distinction between Symbolic stories and Abstraction. So abstraction is not the end game but using symbolic language the writer's message becomes clear.

Hijab Imtiaz: Yes, I agree with you. Abstract is a different thing. They should not be too abstract and even if they are not so abstract that the reader but not so much that one gets lost."

There is a great deal to admire in the above transcript, least of which is Hijab's ability to stand her ground and the beautiful irony of the fact that she mentions an absolutely marvellous Urdu term *dhorak dhanda*, which can be translated into something akin to *a show of some kind to distract, to pull the wool over one's eyes* or *to bamboozle*. She says this in relation to the ability of writer's to use words to do so and it is patently clear from the transcript included that this is exactly what the interviewer is doing, life imitating art indeed.

The Higher Realms of the Imagination

In exactly the same way, I too have delivered light to each individual beat of the heart and it has now become fused within me like an electrical wave. During the monsoon season in subtropical climes, when the soft drops of rain water fall, the Earth accepts them immediately and becomes one with them. In exactly the same manner, I too have become one with the light of your spirit.

The Strings of the Instrument of Life Are Broken, p. 108

From what we can ascertain from the current work we are examining which seems to be a microcosm of the world of Hijab Imtiaz, like those one-off works of fin-de-siècle French writers that seem to be a glimpse into their very soul, is that Hijab Imtiaz was a thinker. Her intellect did not allow her to merely write fiction, but to examine and philosophize on every aspect of the human condition and human existence.

She studied people, her keen faculty of observation is at work in every aspect of her writing, whether it is in describing a character, or the environment in which the character lives. These powers of observation would then be taken to great heights when applied to Nature, Existence, and the Unseen Reality. In *Belles-Lettres*, the Unseen Reality is a form of consciousness in the tradition of great Sufi teachers. She never overtly either wrote of institutional religion, nor did she write against it, as we have seen from the excerpt above from an interview. However, a deep spiritual nature is prevalent throughout, and it is not in her imploring of the Divine Creator in her stories that we are witness to this. It is as if her stories are woven throughout with a deep understanding of the meaning *behind* the meaning. In Sufi terms, the *batin* rather than the *zahir*. Nowhere is this pre-occupation more apparent than in the piece *Posheedgi/ Concealment* (p. 74).

She takes nothing at face value. In the vintage interview with Yousuf Kamran, that we have oft referred to, she describes her deep conviction in the impermanence of all things. In the interview, as Yousuf Kamran grapples with the duality of Hijab's work, he asks:

'How is it,' he asks 'that with your fascination with Nature, there is still a strain of melancholy in your writing. Does Nature not provide humans some respite from sorrow?' To which Hijab replies, 'Yes it is true Nature does give some relief for a little while, but for example even though we are sitting here, I don't know why, instead of feeling full of joy in this gorgeous setting, I see sadness somewhere in the distance . . . even at this moment I am affected by this- even though I am happy that the sky is blue, there is a fountain, butterflies may be dancing, but my sight is always set on our final destination'.[36]

Sufi's talk of *fana-al-fana*, or the dissolution of Self when the Seeker is still in this world but has reached a point where they are lost in the Higher Realms of Consciousness. Most of the stories in *Belles-Lettres* seem to be written from a place of this kind of dissolution. The protagonist is almost always lost

[36] Ibid.

in the seasons, the ocean, the sounds of birds, the small blooms just in their infancy about to appear on the branch of a tree, rain and all that comes with it, the colour of the grass when the summer sun has scorched it all of this and more appears in a kind of whirling dance.

There is also evident a pre-occupation with Eternity as a spiritual state. There are a number of words in the manuscript used for eternity, all describing similar states such as *daimi*, *abdi*, and *baqa*.

The Urdu phrase *kush ma kush* which does not occur in the manuscript is actually very useful in understanding another part of the duality (in itself a Sufic teaching) of Hijab Imtiaz's world. The word describes a kind of tug-of-war as it were—a constant push and pull. This is what we find in *Belles-Lettres*. Life is on one side, but the soul pulls on the rope, yearning for other higher things. Life appears as an inconvenience, and the struggle in her 'I' characters (in that the narration in the short pieces we find in *Belles-Lettres* are almost always in the First Person, which in itself draws the reader into an intimate space).

It appears that what many critics of the time interpreted as sorrow, melancholy, and sadness were not so coloured but rather expressions of existentialism. In this regard too, Hijab was ahead of her time. In *Belles-Lettres* she speaks of notions of power and power seized in the human existence, but she never eschews a Divine Power. That is what sets her apart from Western existentialists and brings her closer to transcendentalists.

We are trying here to put all the different pieces of Hijab together, from various accounts, from her own words and from her works to reach some kind of understanding and consensus of this *rara avis* and her motivations, her interests, and even her practice as a writer.

With her brand of metaphysics, even a devout Buddhist would find a connection with her work. For a Buddhist, silence and stillness are sacred. Observation of Nature, observation of sound, observation of the human experience is part of the spiritual practice. All of which are also Hijab's concerns and what is so compelling about this is that she was intuitively and naturally drawn to these ideals.

She speaks of a desire for silence constantly through her characters. The Urdu word *sakwat*, which is a complex word denoting total absorbing silence appears throughout *Belles-Lettres*. She also mentions often, the character is in solitude, or has been, or is wishing for it, in order to contemplate higher matters:

I have been sitting in this windowsill all morning, contemplating matters of the universe and the arrangement or order of its components while intermittently, you persist in laughing out loud.

Discord, p. 52

A point of note, there are no names in *Belles-Lettres*, and as mentioned the First-Person appears constantly. Hijab's readers often believed that she was writing of herself and her own life, and with this manuscript it is not hard to see why. In fact, it does appear as if it is autobiographical, so intimate and so personal is the work. This is also why, as we have discussed in earlier sections, her work stood apart. It seems in this regard too, the comparison between French autofiction and the Japanese I-novels is closer to what she was doing.

With *Belles-Lettres* it is easy to read the existential dilemmas as Hijab's own, and perhaps they were, but it is a writer's job to above all, create worlds. It is almost irrelevant as to whether they are writing about themselves or not, for ultimately the written work of fiction is a *creation*. In fact, in *Belles-Lettres*, we see a constant battle to assert what 'reality', *is*.

Sufi thought as explained in one of Idries Shah's early works, *The Sufis* at its heart, has this very issue. The way Idries Shah explains it is that in effect, the Sufi must understand that all we see around us is illusion, this also links to the Buddhist notion of *samskara*, some of us may know this as *maya*. So the human is deluded into believing that all that we see and hear and touch is 'reality', where actually it is the Unreality, and all that we *cannot* 'see', with our eyes or experience through our other faculties of sense is in fact the true Reality. For those unfamiliar with this kind of thought, it is an inversion. It is also the deepest truth of the Sufis, one to contemplate and ponder as one continues to work on oneself. These ideas are prevalent throughout *Belles-Lettres*, every person seems to be keenly aware of this, connects with this, *is* this. They *know* this truth in their deepest hearts and live it via their consciousness, as in *The Goat-Herder* (p. 55).

My eyes do not see the glittering electrical lights in the bazaars. My sights are set in the solitary wilds of the forest, seeking the light of destiny. I begin every morning like a story that beckons to one's heart and remain in this state, unaware until the light of the next day hides me in its embrace.

In the world of *Belles-Lettres*, perception is everything.

There are a few other complex Sufi concepts that are also tackled in the book. Such as the beauty of recognition. She talks of *Ishq Pechan*. This is

when you experience a feeling of recognizing someone, but it is in fact Divine recognition. In Sufi philosophy, one is able to *see* the Spirit that connects all of us and you connect with that, when experiencing this mystical state. Rumi's work talked of this constantly, especially in the relationship he would describe with Shams Tabriz. Another complex spiritual idea appears in *Belles-Lettres*—encapsulated very elegantly in Urdu (which is not as elegant when translation is attempted) *Roshan Takhayul*.

We can translate it as bright thinking, bright thoughts but when we contextualize the language with Hijab's metaphysics it is clear the meaning is closer to luminosity and ideas of spirit.

Batin Not Zahir

In general, the al-batin Sufi tradition claims close approaches to the Unseen venerated by the folk belief that their knowledge extends over the apparent worldly affairs to untangle secrets of the Unseen. Sufi leaderships acquire a high status in Muslim societies for they educate the public about the Truth by the spiritual evidence which alone resolves tensions and strains of life.

(Jaafar, 1970; Hassan, 1974)[37]

You will not get a straight answer from the narrator in *Belles-Lettres*. Black is not black and white is not white. The pieces in this collection are at times metaphorical as in the story *The Long Way* (p. 104), symbolic as in *Icy* Hand (p. 60) and philosophically existential as in *Existence* (p. 70):

There is a certain sound that is emitted when the clouds of autumn collide with the mountains.
'What is existence?' they enquire of Nature.
I hear secrets concealed in the formidable crashes of the ocean billows.
I too habitually enquire: 'What is this existence?'
Yes, existence. Your name contains within it burning pain. *Existence, p. 70*

[37] European Scientific Journal June 2016 edition vol.12, No.17 ISSN: 1857–7881 (Print) e - ISSN 1857- 7431, 62 Comparative Research on the Zahir and Batin Thought Mahgoub El-Tigani Mahmoud Sociology, Tennessee State University.

Some pieces take the form of philosophical discourse, sophisticated Socratic dialectic between characters such as in *Concealment* (p. 74). She does not approach life from the outside in, but the inside out. In this way there is layering and complexity in *not-saying* what the narrator wants to say to reveal the hidden (*batin*) behind the 'apparent', or *zahir*. There is no shying away from death in *Belles-Lettres*. At its heart there is a deep understanding of the temporal nature of existence. It reaches extravagant heights in *A Treatise against Eternal Death Inspired by a Shadow* (p. 69):

> If death has any power it will only be able to affect the separation of my
>   spirit from my body and my body from my spirit, much like a rose
>   separated from its branch.
> The following does not strike me as an odd thing to declare:
> Death shall not overcome the aurora of my spirit with engulfing darkness.
> It will never shut down my powers of sight.
> It shall not plunder my sense of self, a living mass of emotions, thoughts
>   and feelings.
> Death shall turn back, confounded upon facing me.

Hijab reaches these dizzying heights of transcendental brilliance often in *Belles-Lettres*. The reader is compelled to be inspired. Such is her power in language. However, the jewel in the crown in this piece is the declaration of immortality that the voice of the piece makes: 'Death shall not overcome the aurora of my spirit with engulfing darkness.'

Just when one feels she cannot outdo herself, a piece such as *Utopia of the Poets* (p. 66), blazes through with the same power. Even more, one might say.

> Comrades—we are all like the bird who wanders these pathways, blind in
> the cruelty of evening. This thing life has done this to us; her restless nature,
> her chaos has impinged on our precious inner bliss, without regard for its
> sanctity.
> Join me in perpetuity. Let us together renounce this artificial world;
> falling prey no longer to her art of deception.

The First-Person voice used in most of the pieces in the collection gives *Belles-Lettres*, feel autobiographical. It is not surprising that critics and readers alike thought she was writing about herself and her own life, but that was apparently not the case—a fact that she has refuted in interviews.

In a review of Aamer Hussein's *Gulmohar Tree*,[38] I speak of his writing in the tradition of Autofiction, a term used in literary criticism to refer to a form of fictionalized autobiography. It was coined in 1977 by Serge Doubrovsky a French writer (later 1989 Prix Médicis winner for Le Livre brisé). He was also a critical theorist, born in 1928 in Paris. He died as recently as 2017.

Autofiction combines two mutually inconsistent narrative forms, namely autobiography and fiction. An author may decide to recount his/her life in the third person, to modify significant details or 'characters', using fiction in the service of a search for self. The Japanese literary tradition has the I-novel,

> The best examples of the genre reflection on personal experience is a vehicle for probing philosophical or social meditation. As the label I-novel suggests, this manner of writing is not simply autobiographical. Writers frequently rework their experience to achieve powerful literary effect, and as in the case of 'The Quilt,' may write in the third person. In most I-novels the distinction between the author and the persona that is the central 'character' remains vague, however.[39]

In a survey of the collection of books of Hijab Imtiaz at her home in Lahore, where she spent her last decade, it is clear she was familiar with French theory and literature, Japanese literature and much more. She and her partner Imtiaz Ali Taj were voracious readers, she was a polymath that much is certain, and her library reflects this. The subject matters vary widely, but most of the library contains first editions of The Maids (Jean Genet), Equus (Peter Shafer), Clinical Aspects of Psychoanalysis (R.LaForgue), Selected Plays of Kuan Han-Ching, Rhinoceros (Eugene Ionesco), Study in Hysteria, How to Be Happy, Lorca, Notes from the Underground (Dosteyovsy), The Seventeenth Doll (summer) and Selected Plays of Euripides, to name a few. However, since the libraries of Taj and Hijab were no doubt shared and so mingles, and because many of the books above were stacked with many, many plays and books about theatre and drama (including Moliere, Wilde, Nell Simon), we cannot say definitively exactly which books she personally had engaged with.

She stands easily alongside the French and Japanese traditions, as her own representative of her very own tradition.

---

[38] Herald Magazine, Karachi August 2009.
[39] The 'I' Novels in the Context of Early 20th-Century Japan—Japan Society Teacher's Resource.

'Hijab was not interested in what form the writing came out, she just wrote. She was a truly free spirit'[40]

It did not matter to her whether people thought her work was autobiographical or not. 'I do not write for an audience. I write for myself, and if people enjoy what I write than I am fortunate, if not neither am, I concerned.'[41]

In India, contemporary autofiction has been associated with the works of Hainsia Olindi and postmodern Tamil writer Charu Nivedita. His novel Zero degree, a ground-breaking work in Tamil literature and his recent Novel *Marginal Man* are examples of this genre. Japanese author Hitomi Kanehara wrote a novel titled *Autofiction*.

The works of Rahman Abbas are generally considered works of autofiction especially his two novels 'Nakhalistan Ki Talash' (Search of an Oasis) and 'Khuda Ke Saaye Mein Ankh Micholi' (Hide & Seek in the Shadow of God).

For Hijab, writing was not an extension of herself, as it *was* her. It was her natural state. She started as early back as she can remember, and apart from half a decade when she was mourning for her husband, she wrote till the very end of her days. She stood as a literary canon in herself.

Form aside, the content of her work has an astounding mobility of thought. She applies scale to her perspective. At times as in *Heat*, and *Autumn Leaf*— we are zoomed into a moment, in great depth. At other times we are zoomed out. Consciousness is at work, and themes of the intrinsic Buddhist duality between Thought (Mind) and Consciousness are constant. The narrator(s) struggle; memories are a burden:

> I succumbed to the past. One memory in particular, heady and electric, yet so very bittersweet . . . my heart felt made of the most fragile of glasses, cracking to bits upon recalling it. I sensed my spirit unable to bear this burden of unbidden memory, parting from my body as I saw an image emerge of you and I, five years earlier.
>
> Missing Pages from the Book of Life (p. 72)

In Monsoon (p. 89) the natural world is a catalyst to an abduction by memory:

> You may well find yourself rooted to the spot, hours pass, you wouldn't know, propelled as you are into the realm of dream, watching images of old

---

[40] Translator's interview with Yasmine and Naeem Tahir in their home; Lahore 2019.
[41] Interview 1 Lutfullah Archives 2018.

and hearing melodies of yore. For a spirit inclined to fancy, it is a time of intensity & passion.

Nowhere is a Buddhist ideal more prevalent than in On Thought (p. 73):

When the Spirit, naturally inclined to silent contemplation is meditating in peace in some wilderness of Mind's creation, he appears, presenting the sound and fury of wartime, in an effort to wilfully create disturbance. It works.

The narrator often struggles with a need to just *be*. She (as the narrator is most often female) doesn't want to be disturbed by life, as she finds life quite disturbing. In Conversation with a Girlfriend (p. 56) a nameless narrator is engaged in a conversation with her friend:

I say to you—this life which you & I believe so dear is a thing of chaos and fury, is it not? We find ourselves facing terrifying breakers rising as if from the sea and obstacles that spring up immobile like mountains.

Both people close to her and literary thinkers have spoken of her as an 'escapist', but that is not our concern. As the reader, we are willing to escape with her.

Her work can be didactic, and familiar with Greek oration. The reader might find herself embarking with the narrator on a philosophical argument as in Autumn Leaf or in The Sea, a poem written 'in response to Frederick George Scott's Little River', and by the end of it, she has won you over.

So persuasive is her argument, calling on the spirits of Nature, the elements, the seasons, the birds to back her point in a kind of Shamanic oratorial monologue. Hijab manages to have you on her team, and she is a master of turning you to her logic and then you are in her world haplessly.

In a work such as Treatise on Eternal Death Inspired by a Shadow (p. 69), her grip of ideas of consciousness is on par with works of Western philosophy. The narrator believes that the true *I* or *you* does not reside in the body, but can travel anywhere, anytime.

My spirit shall reside forevermore smiling out behind the stars. Let the open sky of my life be marred by death-clouds and my body vanish from sight like the stars obscured by cloud. My spirit will remain unchanged; a light amongst lights rejoicing.

The famous Dylan Thomas poem Death Shall Have No Dominion comes to mind:

> And death shall have no dominion.
> No more may gulls cry at their ears
> Or waves break loud on the seashores;
> Where blew a flower may a flower no more
> Lift its head to the blows of the rain;
> Though they be mad and dead as nails,
> Heads of the characters hammer through daisies;
> Break in the sun till the sun breaks down,
> And death shall have no dominion.

The unnamed narrator(s)in *Belles-Lettres* do not believe that death has any dominion over them.

Psychogeography and Aesthetics

The title *Belles-Lettres* has been translated as such because the slim volume Hijab published early in her career reflects the French tradition of 'Beautiful Letters', or a kind of refined writing—'literature that is an end in itself and not merely informative *specifically*: light, entertaining, and often sophisticated literature.'[42]

There is attention to detail in every story, and Hijab emerges as a time keeper. With her, we follow the passage of time via the seasons. At times we are with her characters experiencing the heady romance of spring and witnessing new growth.

> I am convinced that when the fragrant spring breeze causes a clamour when dishevelling the leaves on the branches of trees, she is whispering secrets of her love.
>
> The Poet Wishes (p. 103)

The drama of Nature affects her character(s), the psychogeography of *Belles-Lettres* is derived from this.

---

[42] Merriam-Webster, 11th Edition, 2020.

Come spring, the elegant red flowers of the trumpet vine open themselves up on each and every branch to the brilliant rays of sunlight. In order to flourish and restore their glory they allow the vitality of the light to reach inside them and are keen to take in the reinvigorating air of spring.

The Strings of the Instrument of Life Are Broken (p. 108)
There are 22 mentions of autumn in Belles-Lettres. The wisdom that the characters have to relay is often wrapped up in the mysteries of the season. Awareness of death in life that is the very bedrock of the volume is constantly reiterated via the season of autumn as in Icy Hand (p. 60):

Dearest have you noticed the state of the trees in autumn? How they stand lost and abandoned. Their leaves desiccated. No life is left in them. None. Springs dry up and are bereft of their musical waters.

Or as in Raison D'Etre (p. 87):

A deathly silence was upon us. It was one of those evenings in autumn when it was easy to feel unhappy. From deep in the valleys, the continuous yearning crowing of roosters, echoes.

In summer, the majesty of Nature seems to reach a visceral peak. Hijab reminds her reader of the intensity of the heat in the sub-tropical climes she is writing about. The heat is often the only thing that is being experienced on every level. This is perhaps wrought most masterfully in Advent of Afternoon (p. 110):

The exhilarating light of the sun, falling on the leaves of the banana plant, causes them to glow. Colossal deserts, endless fields and soaring mountain ranges all transform into a blaze of fire in the noonday sun while miniature birds seek protection in the olive groves and poppy shrubs, weakened by the intensity of the heat.

In Young Ascetic (p. 85), the narrator asks the question of how the Man of Contemplation is able to endure the severity of the heat:

The heat of eastern climes is known to take lives and wear away at souls. Does your body which seems made of marble not feel it?

In terms of literary precedence—the fine brush strokes, the often fleeting subject matter, the disregard for conforming to any particular genre or trope, the pre-occupation with beautiful things, the wry, fearless observations have more in common with the seminal work *The Pillow Book* of a certain Sei Shōnagon.

'How far has this text travelled since Sei Shônagon took up her brush, let her mind hover on the elegant and intriguing question of what moment of the day most quintessentially matches the feeling of spring, and pictured that moment when dawn has begun to whiten the sky behind the dark line of the mountains, as she wrote those words a thousand years ago? Surely it has travelled quite as far as it must travel to reach us in the translated words "In spring, the dawn—when the slowly paling mountain rim is tinged with red." '

McKinney, Meredith; Kyoto Journal 2011

Sei Shōnagon was a lady of the court who served the Empress Teishi around the year 1000 who became known as a Japanese author and poet. In *The Pillow Book*, the language is considered to be the 'epitome of classical beauty, the more beautiful for being more or less incomprehensible'.[43] The lofty themes in Hijab's work could be also considered more or less incomprehensible at times, and the language is most definitely a perfect example set in time of a clean, simple but complex and poetic lexicon. The Urdu of Hyderabad Deccan.

Like Hijab Imtiaz, who possessed knowledge of a vast array of world poetries, theatre, and other literatures, Sei Shōnagon possessed a deep knowledge of Japanese and Chinese poetry. They both shared a quick tongue and a keen eye.

Hijab may not have created lists such as Shōnagon, who was known for such whimsies as 'Things That Make the Heart Beat Faster', 'Occasions When Time Drags By', 'Things That Are Far yet Near' ('Relations between men and women') but her concerns were very much similar. Including the complete immersion in her environment and the world around.

Hijab's brand of aesthetic shares concerns with other Japanese writers. In Japanese society, there is a great prevalence of *Shinto*, 'followers draw their deities from nature—worshipping the rocks, trees, wind, and sun. Dwarfed

---

43   Kyoto Journal *The Pillow Book: Translating a Classic* 28 June 2011 Meredith McKinney.

by nature, Shinto shrines provide a sense of calm. Set within beautiful gardens, these sacred places venerate the spirits of the natural world'.[44]

There is a strong sense of the near-worship of Nature in *Belles-Lettres*. One could easily make a case for Hijab being as comfortable in the Japanese literary scene as a Japanese reader would be reading her work.

Japanese culture also has at its heart the complex and yet simple values of *Wabi-Sabi*; which simply translated as finding beauty in things that are broken or considered 'ugly'. For the discerning reader, there are many instances of this kind of thinking. In *Missing Pages from the Book of Life* (p. 72) a landscape with cacophonous bird sounds and layers of melancholy, there is beauty everywhere:

> On the monumental trees in the cemetery, doves cried. Parrots of the sea and mountain myna screamed out from ocean passageways. The winds whipping up forced the mightiest of almond and fig trees to sway and bend, kiss the ground and rise again with each gust. Other songs were layered into this soundscape; the songs of the fishermen and wayfarers. Everything spelt tragedy.

Broken strings of instruments are also a favourite with Hijab alongside Socratic dialogue concerning deep philosophical thought experiments similar to, 'If a tree falls in a forest and no one is around to hear it, does it make a sound?' In Concealment (p. 74) the narrator's friend asks:

> my dear soul—have you not contemplated this: In the depth of Midwinter when people are shivering in the cold of December, huddled around fires, that luminous object exalted by poets rises in the night sky and all comes alive in diamond light. But it makes no difference whether entire valleys are sparkling in this light or towering mountains ... for there is no-one there to see them. I ask you then, does the beauty vanish like the brilliance of a gemstone that sinks in the ocean?

In the piece entitled *Song* (p. 57), there is an intense beauty to a description filled with sorrow:

---

[44] Shinto: Nurturing Nature; BBC World Service 2011.

In the solitude of night—far off a bulbul sitting on a branch of the night-blooming jasmine too was singing her song. To me, it sounded like Nature was sobbing, taking loud intakes of breaths—emitting 's' sounds softly.

Hijab Imtiaz's investment in the lament is note-worthy. She continually finds ever more reasons and ways in which *to* lament. When she takes you for a 'spin', she manages to bring you in for a landing as well. In *The Strings of the Instrument of Life Are Broken* her lament is that of a true existentialist. It is a treatise on our complete lack of control as human beings. By the end of the piece it is hard not to see the tragedy of this.

Perhaps one day this world will be destroyed, and I will be left standing here, defeated, on the threshold to Imagination, in the form of a fakir, with the demeanour of a beggar.

As discussed, Hijab was not limited by form. Some of the works in *Belles-Lettres* are like works of Dutch Realist painters. The piece *Flaxen Hair* is replete with attention to light, contrast between dark and light and exteriors and interiors.

All her varying powers come together in the piece *A Poet Wishes*. It is as if the collection reaches a crescendo. All the elements and symbols throughout the book are present in the piece; thunderstorms, the moon, winds, repetition of themes like music. It is as if the book has been scored and each element or symbol, a note, and with *A Poet Wishes*, it reaches its zenith.

Form and 'Form-ability'

Towards the end of the manuscript and in a few earlier tracts Hijab assigns her own categorization to the pieces. These categorizations are like a key to her singular poetics for her reader. So, the piece *Flaxen Hair* is assigned the sub-title: 'Nazm Numa Nasr' as is the piece *The Last Evening*. In investigating these titles, which are very much Hijab's own, it is not clear what she means. *Flaxen Hair* as mentioned is representational in its form and is written in prose structure.

The term Nazm Numa Nasr seems to mean many things. Nazm in Urdu has the meaning of an arrangement, like stringing pearls, and is used as a word for poem. Numa Nasr is *resembling composition or prose*. *The Last Evening* is in fact very much a work of prose.

Turning our attention to her other categorization: 'Sher Mansoor', there is a similar discrepancy between what we as readers may understand and what the writer means. The piece *Song* and *The Advent of Evening* are both given the sub-title Sher Mansoor. In this case, *Song* is very much a work of prose in structure. Sher—literally means a verse, while mansoor also has the meaning of scattered like a pearl, when used as an adjective, while *The Advent of Evening* is the only piece in *Belles-Lettres* that has a formal verse structure (Sher), with a refrain. Both pieces are very different from each other but definitely the assessment can be made that they are more 'poetic', thematically.

Certainly, in *Song* which she assigns the label of prose-poem to there is a form change. The flow is continuous with very long sentence structures but just to throw us off a little more she has named the piece 'Geet' or Song. Now this may encourage a reader to decide this is in fact a song but upon working with it and keeping in mind her own categorization it is probably closer to the truth that it is a prose poem that is about song.

In my interview with them, asmine and Naeem Tahir verify that these assignations were totally of Hijab's own creation.

We can use these 'keys', if we so wish to 'unlock', the segments that have not been assigned these keys which ultimately act as an insight into the writer's methods, techniques, and practice. They appear almost as notes to herself but give so much rich sub-text to the reading that one cannot help but wish she had assigned more, but also it does ask the question as to why some over others?

And what did she then consider the other pieces? Surely, they all teeter on the brink of 'prose-poem'? The one that lends the most compelling insight is Nazm Numa Nasr. This work of hers heralds a kind of turning away from impressionism as she calls it Representational and yet it most certainly does hold within it the strokes of impression certainly it is not an internalized 'expression'—also the word, nazm here is telling, as in the other pieces she uses the term sher which means verse—this signifies an important distinction.

Final Chapters in the Book of Life

After enduring the violent experience in her home, in her own bed resulting in Imtiaz Ali Taj's death and a permanent scar in the area of her heart, Hijab did retire from life for a while, choosing as one critic put it to 'be an observer and not a participant in society'.

It appears though that the literary community rallied around her and continued to give her support in what surely must have been troubled times. Begum Almas Daulata, the wife of political figure Mian Mumtaz Daulatana who supported the Pakistan Movement in British India, Lady Zulfikar Ali Khan and Hijab were great friends. Hijab began to curate a monthly event in her home. The event was called Mann-o-Salva (Gift from the Gods) and was attended by the literary community.

Even in this regard, Hijab did things differently. There was no great buffet or banquet served up by domestic staff, as one may imagine to be the case at a gathering such as this. Everyone was asked to bring their own foods and everyone would sit down and eat together, not just exchanging ideas, thought and stories but also various kinds of cuisine.

Besides the victuals, anyone who wanted to read a new story would do so. Hijab often read her new stories. Her literary salon was a hot-bed of discussion. There is no doubt a lofty roster for these salons, if we were to delineate a list, some of those people included Jameela Hashmi, Ahmed Nadeem Qasmi, and Salah-ud-deen Mahmud, all feted Urdu writers at the time.

As discussed earlier on in this essay, in describing her childhood to critic Intezar Hussein, Hijab spoke of 'flowers, of kokilas, of riverbanks, the banks of the Godawari and Krishna, of mango-trees, and of the rainy season', but she also revealed that 'at home I had 28 cats around me'. This seemed to be a recurring theme in her life, soon after setting up home with Imtiaz Ali Taj, she also managed to accumulate the same number of cats in her environs. It is said that she worked on her editorial duties, her own writing and in addition 'personally attended to the cats'.

'Siamese cats are much admired. But I tell you that they in general are dull and unintelligent. As compared to them the cats wandering in our lanes and streets are by the grace of God very sensible, intelligent and wise.'[45]

It seems after the tragedy she suffered, she no longer had cats around her and is reported to have said, 'I am now a tired woman. I can't look after them properly', when asked why this was. By another account however, towards the end of her life, she did have close to a dozen cats and parrots in what the writer termed her 'Ajaib Khana', a term which is closer to cabinet of curiosities than anything else, but literally means Weird or Strange Space.

She lived till the age of 93, and even though she took some time out for grieving, it is quite clear that she did not ever stop writing. In fact, the

[45]   Excerpt from transcript of interview between Intezar Hussein and Hijab Imtiaz Ali Taj.

evolution that she talks about as being necessary and at times not even a choice, for writers, as the times change was possibly what kept her going.

The intense period of science-based research she undertook for the novel Pagal Khana[46] was done during this time. As a highly sensitive individual, she was obviously affected by the terrifying intimations of Nuclear armament, that had begun to emerge on the world scene. As a result of this sensitivity, she chose to tackle this subject, completely out of her comfort zone and perhaps in the case of this novel she deviated a little from her own maxim, that fiction should not be for social commentary. However, it was a groundbreaking novel, perhaps again ahead of its time and certainly the first and only by an Urdu writer, and most definitely by a woman writer. This was to be her last novel.

In the later interviews referenced her that have recently emerged from the Lutfullah archives, the timbre of her voice changes, and her curious high lilt is no longer there as she became a grandmother, a great grandmother living on until she was 92. Those interviews are very special for this reason, as they are the last, she may have done that this writer is aware of at the time of writing this.

In her answers put forward by the interviewer, there may be more pauses, and some parts which are harder to parse as it is obviously a little difficult for her to enunciate, but there is no change in her sharp intellect, her clarity in her beliefs as a writer, her sense of self, her memory of her work and what she has achieved.

When the interviewer asks her about writing in Urdu she speaks as always with grace and elegant turn of phrase while making it clear she disagrees with what he is saying.

If we divide Hijab's life into three main stages—Childhood/Pre-Lahore, Lahore, and last of all, Post-tragedy, we can chart the spectrum of her life. Post-Tragedy Hijab's life was distinct from the other phases. Naeem Tahir played a great part in it. As discussed earlier, he blended naturally with the family. He has a background in psychology and that coupled with his own devotion and loyalty to the family, led him to the conclusion that the family should travel.

Hijab, Yasmine, and the Tahir sons, Mehran, Faran, and Ali, went to the United Kingdom for a while. 'I felt that this was the way to help with the healing, after what Hijab and of course, Yasmine had suffered, and I knew it

---

[46] Idara Taj-o-Hijab, Lahore, 1980.

would take some time,'[47] what is remarkable is that he took it on himself to facilitate the process of healing. They got rid of the house where the incident took place, as mentioned he resigned from his job. In order to support the family he then went into a completely different field—the carpet business. All these actions and more were taken for the family.

Escaping the terrible memories of the past, the family remained abroad for a while. They lived in California as well. 'Bibi (Hijab)did not write for about four to five years', Yasmine and Naeem share, but they both also relate with a kind of pride, that return to some semblance of her old life, she did.

Naeem is grateful that his carpet business took off. He was then able to build a new home in Lahore for Yasmine and Hijab, and the children. It is clear they were a close-knit unit. 'Mehran (the middle son of Yasmine and Naeem), was especially close to Bibi', his mother relates. 'Bibi would go out to visit friends or for some kind of outing and Mehran would always be keen to go with her and Bibi would love to have him along.'[48]

Nothing about Hijab was obvious or predictable, neither her work, nor her life, as we have been examining. 'For example, in her daily life, she often preferred out-of-the-way, simple eateries. She could have gone to say the big hotels, such as Faletti's and so forth, but she would tell Mehran to come along, and take him to a small restaurant with good food. They would then order to eat in the car on trays,'[49] as much as she could have basked in the spotlight, which she surely was in and out of, she preferred to shun it.

Her daughter intimated that the Mann-O-Salva event was to become a great source of comfort and healing for her mother. 'She would get very excited and look forward to every event, and plan what they would discuss.' It was held in the house that her daughter and son-in-law currently live in. The drawing room where the greater part of this salon took place is still the same as it was when Hijab hosted her event. Her upright piano sits in a corner, which she played from time to time.

The walls are adorned with exquisite pieces of original artwork. In particular, three pieces by Abdur Rahman Chugtai draw one in. A tall etching in a vertical frame adorns the far north wall. It is almost Chinese in its style, with two gazelles with long, delicate horns beneath a tall tree. Even before Yasmine Tahir shares its provenance, it calls to mind the mise-en-scene's in Hijab's works. One can well imagine, Hijab with her penchant for high art

---

[47] Interview with Yasmine and Naeem Tahir in their home, 2019.
[48] Ibid.
[49] Ibid.

staring into this image for hours on end. Which it is then made clear that she probably did as this was a wedding present given to her and Taj by Chughtai. The other two Chugtai's equally compelling and finely wrought and obviously from a later decade were gifts for the wedding of Yasmine and Naeem. Within this same living room, other pointers to Hijab emerge. A beautiful cat comes running through, a gentle dog potters in and out. Hijab's family intimate jokingly, that they are very suspicious of people who either do not like animals or treat animals badly. This was also Hijjab's legacy. She had a pet monkey as well, that she had to find a new home for at some point. 'She went and found a place for her monkey in a zoo at the time, with the warning that they must take care of it, as it was like her own family. She would then continue to visit the monkey for quite some time,' Yasmine tells us.

Hijab had some lung complications; the cause of her death. She did not suffer very long and passed away just short of the 21st century in 1999. Imtiaz Ali Taj had been buried in one of Lahore's oldest cemeteries the *Mominpura* graveyard, The Mominpura Graveyard is a Shia cemetery in Lahore, Pakistan. It is one of the oldest graveyards in Lahore and contains over 10,000 burials according to its records. Many graves are hundreds of years old. Several other notable individuals are buried there, also.

A Note

I have conducted interviews of authors for print publications in my career. I am also a poet, fiction writer, educator, and above all student of the great mysteries. I made the careful choice to write this essay in a style that may not be common in this kind of work. What I have created is a syncretic scholarship style comprising primary sources from the author herself, and a poet's commentary and analysis (mine) of the translated work. I allow Hijab Imtiaz to mostly speak for herself, because that material was newly available and has not been utilized. My modus operendi has been to present her as human and not couch her ineffable being in heavy literary garb in a manner that *obscures* the person and her journey.

The areas I have spent time on were chosen from what I believe to be important *to the author*. She did not care for the external world. She was a hermit on so many levels. I have spent time in the essay on her personal relationship because it *was* pivotal to her life and work and the brutal death of her partner affected her hugely. I have also, however, been keen to show her *in her own light*. In the existing narratives, she is often placed in the shadow

of Imtiaz Ali Taj and her father, the aristocrat. I have found this remiss and have strived with this essay to illuminate *her* life independent of the wider patriarchal system.

This has been a primary concern. I also feel strongly that her work has been largely misunderstood, and it is to this end that I have laboured at widening the scope of her work beyond the Subcontinent. I myself have studied Japanese Literature, French Literature, and Buddhist thought—what I have found in *Belles-Lettres* continues to be a source of astonishment and delight. I am not imposing a Western context on her arbitrarily by any means. There is a definite correspondence and this is what I want anyone interested in Hijab Imtiaz to learn from my book.

My research methodology has involved seeking out obscure articles and audio interviews never translated before as I believe this kind of primary source material is key to a 'truer' understanding of the personage that she was. To this end, I have included a transcript of a never-before translated video interview[50] which I found to be utterly memorable and of a rare quality.

Ultimately, conducting interviews with her closest remaining family members, visiting the house she died in, being able to observe her remarkable library of world thought and literature, examine her personal effects, including a beloved collection of statues from diverse spiritual branches and hold in my hands and read her diaries gave me the most confidence in all my decisions as editor, writer, translator, and as a poet. The effect I suppose could be said to be anthropological.

I feel humbled and grateful to be able to do this author and thinker justice and I am glad to be able to bring my own specific syncretic poet's sensibility to the translation. I feel that this is important to mention here.

I am above all, a poet. I am known as a poet. This work is, therefore, the work above all—of a poet honouring another poet.

Transcending that it is also a document of my own experience of Ishq Pehchan in the life and work of Begum Hijab Imtiaz—from one seeker to others.

Sascha Akhtar
London, January 2022

---

[50] Yousuf Kamran interview PTV show Dastan Go, 1964.

BELLES-LETTRES

Translated from original Urdu title Adab-E-Zareen

Belles-Lettres. Sascha A. Akhtar, Oxford University Press. © Oxford University Press India 2022.
DOI: 10.1093/oso/9780190132644.003.0002

Desiderations	51	Separation	79
Discord	52	That Unforgettable Morning	80
Fear	53	The Fantastic Luck of Travellers	82
Three Questions	54	Your Call in the Wild; the	
The Goat-Herder	55	Imaginings of a Girl Cutting	
Conversation with a Girlfriend	56	Wheat in the Fields	84
Song	57	Young Ascetic	85
Love of Another	58	The Sleep of the Bulbul	86
Yearning	59	Raison D'Etre	87
Icy Hand	60	An Afternoon in Summer	88
Je Ne Sais Quois	62	Monsoon	89
True Happiness	63	The Spirit of Cupid	92
One Morning in Autumn	64	Fascination	95
The Advent of Afternoon	65	Addressing the Poet	96
Utopia of the Poets:	66	Ray of Pure Light	97
The Heat	68	When I Get the Blues	98
Treatise against Eternal Death		During the Monsoon,	
Inspired by a Shadow	69	the Westering Sun	100
Existence	70	The Sea	101
Ma Chérie Écoute	71	The Poet Wishes	103
Missing Pages from the Book of Life	72	The Long Way	104
On Thought	73	Flaxen Hair	106
Concealment	74	Song	107
Prayer	76	The Strings of the Instrument of Life	
An Autumn Leaf	77	Are Broken	108
Simplicity	78	The Advent of Evening	110
		The Last Evening	111

Desiderations

On the horizon, the sun continues to drown.

And with it my desiderations, wretched as they are, sink. The sun's return tomorrow is assured. My longings lost and forgetful will wander off. Again, the sun will rise. They will have set with lasting effect, never to return. In the forest, deer stray onto paths unknown, yet return to their base instinctually. My wishes seem to no longer recognize the way home and are doomed to roam, lost.

Friend, my sweet, sweet friend, watch how slowly the sun is setting and with it my desires, wretched as they are, sink. They are drowning, never to emerge again.

Today this too has been erased. Another story ends.
The mark of wanting, a wish to remember.

Discord

I have been sitting on this windowsill all morning, contemplating matters of the universe and the arrangement or order of its components while intermittently, you continue to laugh out loud.

A bumblebee singing its raga comes buzzing through my window. It lifts my spirits immensely, but your face reddens with anger as you set about agitated by its presence, to end its life.

Enough! I feel exhausted by this discord life feels imbued with venom. The constant rumination on worldly matters leads me astray from my true purpose.

And you, you lift your head, as if enraptured by some great delights.

Fear

Opposing winds are blowing so fiercely, I am afraid they might uproot my wish-tree.

Three Questions

I am addressing you, the blooms of my deepest
Wishes. Why have you withered away while the
Roses in the gardens are vivacious, still. Cool
Morning dew has teased open their petals.

I suppose hot tears do not do the same.

I address you, the moon of my deepest wishes.
I cannot see you, hidden away. The moon
In the sky seems to have risen out of the
Tumult of winter clouds. Will you
Never sparkle on the sky of joy?

You, the fields of my deepest wishes, why
Do you lie dry and barren? Will you not
Grow and wave your grasses in the air of
Contentment and tranquility?

The monsoons have rendered the fields
Of wheat lush and verdant. Were the
Clouds of virtue and contentment
Unable to water you back to life?

The Goat-Herder

Which ragas do the creatures of the city sing, I couldn't tell you. I read the poem of my life sitting beneath lazuline skies in the shade of date palms and mulberry trees. I do not hear the superficial laughter echoing from the dwellings. Disengaged from the spectacle of life, day and night, in a pure reverie I remain at one with a smile that has its roots deep within.

My eyes do not see the glittering electrical lights in the bazaars. My sights are set in the solitary wilds of the forest, seeking the light of destiny. I begin every morning like a story that beckons to one's heart and remain in this state, unaware until the light of the next day hides me in its embrace.

The denizens of the world, dread awakening from sleep and greeting the morning of their lives. From fitful sleep they awake, absorbing the troubles of the day into their very breath like the poison of a mighty snake. Come nightfall, how is it I, the goat-herder smile in my slumber while the leaders of the world sigh through their suffering sleep exhausted from the nightmares of their day.

Which ragas are these the creatures of the city sing, I couldn't tell you.

Conversation with a Girlfriend

I say to you—this life which you and I believe so dear is a thing of chaos and
fury, is it not? We find ourselves facing terrifying breakers rising as if
from the sea and obstacles that spring up immobile like mountains.

Yes, this life, that you and I thought such a perfectly wrought bud, seems
more like a tree under the ravages of autumn; at times dry, at others
struggling to burst back into life.

This life—that you and I thought would bring us so much is proving to be a
destructive force for me; a kind of poison that kills you slowly while
you are still living.

This life—which you and I thought of as the benevolent dream manifestation
of an angel, is the eternal laughter of the Devil.

This life—which we would give rosaries of light to, is a star that has burst and
broken away from the cosmos giving no indication as to where it
has vanished.

And despite all this—my friend—despite all this, I really cannot understand
why the human race perceives this existence of ours as Nature's su-
perior contrivance.

Song

In the darkest recesses of night, I sat on my windowsill composing a poem. Near my window, a playful bee born of summer sang a full-throated song. I heard not a song, but someone in the celestial chambers, praying for an end to their suffering.

I began to compose the second verse of my poem.

The clear summer sky appeared to sparkle with points of light. Under the shade of the stars, a passer-by wandering was lost in a raga of his own. It was as if the sound of a waterfall was emanating from the realm of Poetry and Song.

I began the fourth verse of my poem.

In the solitude of night, far off a bulbul sitting on a branch of the night-blooming jasmine too was singing her song. To me, it sounded like Nature was sobbing, taking loud intakes of breaths, emitting soft 's' sounds.

I had finished my poem.

Love of Another

Her face looked deathly pale. I was concerned and so I spoke:

If all it causes is dejection and nothing else, then throw love out of the order of things! Love of the Other appears to have one objective only; to cause abjection in life. It has not given rise to anything beautiful in the history of human civilisation. It causes rifts and fights. Let us throw it out of the canon of poetry! Look. Read the verses with care and whenever you sense the tender allure of love, end it there and then!

She didn't seem to take my words too well. She appeared a wraith, wan and lost, that has descended into the garden with the help of the celestial lights in the atmosphere of night.

'How do you propose we live in such darkness then?' she said, 'What is the purpose of the frenetic motion of life? You say you are able to live in the darkness of night without a guiding light but what is the purpose of that life? You will neither be able to read, nor, you lunatic, will you be able to see that your Book of Music has many more, new songs for you'.

I had to smile at her words. I pulled my silk, cerulean blue shawl embossed with ships around my shoulders. That evening she had illuminated love with a rare light. I was amused.

Yearning

Behind the grape vines, when the red sun sets my gaze begins to search.

Abashed, I hide in the protective shelter of the mountains but there too the white chrysanthemums reflect your visage.

Perhaps this is yearning. Everything large or small under the sun reminds me of your grandeur.

When my dark eyes rest upon the star-encrusted night, the midnight-blue of the sky and the shine of the stars; your eyes appear before me filled with tears of joy.

At twilight, in my chambers I stand at the open window. The sun appears emerald, with the colour of the thickets of acacia it sets behind. Its rays reminding me of your hair, almost orange in hue.

Dear one, this is one of those times when my yearning for you is a cause of great heartache for me.

Icy Hand

Friend, what is it you are seeking with your hands outstretched? A thing once lost is not to be found. A thing that is gone will not come back.

You tell me, have gusts of wind ever turned around? Do autumn leaves return once withered away? What then is it you are seeking with your hands outstretched? There is not a thing here, that you are searching for.

Dearest, her icy hands have turned the burning coals of sweet warm love, ice cold. She has felled incredible soldiers, the bravest of hearts and strong, weathered bodies in the manner a tornado would uproot weak plants. Why do you continue to search? The place you seek will not here be found.

Have you not observed how the luminous smile of a child, so trusting, can be transformed into permanent stillness or drowned into the everlasting silence of illness? Faces reddened by life, overcast by a withering chill. Why, then do you continue this fruitless restlessness? The place you seek does not exist here.

Have you not wondered how, when evening arrives, the mighty sun sets? At their appointed time, even the stars are dulled and disappear—Do the ocean waves not fade out of existence once they reach the shore?

Here, nothing is established, stable, immortal. Why then do you fret and fiddle? The place you seek does not exist here. You will not stay safe here. It does not matter whether you hide beneath the blinds or deadbolt the door of your house or grab onto your lover and refuse to let go.

Have you not noticed how bright and clear her eyes glow? She has kissed the foreheads of the grand residents of mansions. Her bare hands break down the strongest doors. Her sharp eyes can find those hiding in the darkness. Her swift steps can scale the tops of treacherous mountains and castles in the sky. Tell me, what is it you are seeking with your hands outstretched? The place you seek does not exist here.

Dearest, have you noticed the state of the trees in autumn? How they stand lost and abandoned. Their leaves desiccate. No vitality remains. None. Springs dry up and are bereft of their musical waters.

Everything vanishes at an appointed time. Multi-hued panoplies of cloud, too dissipate in the winds. The song of the bulbul once mingled dies down to silence in the winds and the strings of the lute too are defeated. Nothing lives forever.

Aye. Nothing. What then is it you are seeking with your hands outstretched? The place you seek does not exist here.

Look at the evolution of the land. Over the course of centuries, the oceans, too, are forced to leave their positions. The most majestic of gardens can turn to desolate ruins on the turn of a pin. The pages of time keep turning. They cannot be stopped.

By the same token, I fear you disappearing from the space you occupy in life. And it is also possible that I go far away and, upon returning, do not find my friend anywhere. Or what if I stayed home and my friend went on a journey, and upon returning found me gone?

Why then do you keep seeking with your hands outstretched? The place you seek is not here.

Creatures of Adam, see how, every day the Angel of Death comes towards our wellspring of vitality, with her arms wide open. One day her icy hands will extinguish this fire, too.

Je Ne Sais Quois

At eventide, I am driven to enquire: What mysterious force is it that makes lucent the physiognomy of the farmer in the gloaming?

At the appointed time, shadows of the clementine and tangerine trees flutter on the clear surface of the freshwater river.

In the temples of the Divine the flames of the lanterns awaken. At a loss, what remains of daylight wanders perplexed like a traveller who strays first one way, then the other before she vanishes altogether in some mysterious westerly ravine.

What remains of evening? What is it that lights up the faces of fatigued labourers, weary from the day's toils?

What is this thing?

True Happiness

Dear one you smile with such ease. I, on the other hand, feel out-of-sorts and have no idea where my happiness lies.

How do you receive happiness?

I witnessed a distraught bumble-bee, trapped in my windowsill clumsily clambering, trying to find its way. It was clear that for this creature true happiness was close by—if it could just get there to the garden of intoxicating scents.

What is unclear to me is where my happiness has been sequestered.

A brisk night in autumn sees a child with his sights fixed on the sky but the unforgiving clouds do not allow him a glimpse of the elusive moon. His eyelashes glisten with the tears welling up. It is not long before the fast-moving winds of the same inclement weather blow those clouds away. The moon, victorious appears smiling, a smile reflected back in the face of the boy.

It is hard for me to comprehend how people find this pure happiness so readily.

The lively, young lotus flowers in the pond appear to banter back and forth while in the forests, I hear the sounds of joy in the whistles of the birds. From in between the delicate blades of viridian grass the restless toads begin their celebrations.

I address you, the Divine Architect: There are so many fascinating, peculiar ways that have been devised to receive true happiness. I regret I am frightfully unaware of these things and I know not where my joy lies concealed.

Will you set off with me, dearest? Together, let us uncover the hiding place of our bliss.

One Morning in Autumn

That morning a beige pallor hung over her countenance. I felt the winds were singing a dirge, emanating from the dark depths of a remote cave.

I did not speak, nor did she make any effort to do so. It was as if we were in silent agreement that a morning such as this did not warrant conversation between two people who love. I spent most of the day counting the thrashing, mottled breakers from my window, perched on the window-sill.

She sat on the couch, silently, making attempts to pry music from the distressed strings of her lute.

The Advent of Afternoon

The noonday sun throws spirited shafts of light into my courtyard, dispelling all darkness. The clouds decamp to distant shores. The banana plants, blooming, nourished by the spirit of the southerly winds, dance.

Storms hide away in the depths of the oceans. Not a vestige of turbulence remains, anywhere. The only sound, the roar of autumnal storm clouds in the outlying mountains.

The exhilarating light of the sun, falling on the leaves of the banana plant, causes them to glow. Colossal deserts, endless fields, and soaring mountain ranges all transform into a blaze of fire in the noonday sun while miniature birds seek protection in the olive groves and poppy shrubs, weakened by the intensity of the heat.

In the forests too, the lions and stag with twelve horns, fevered, hasten back and forth to drink from the springs.

I, stand silently for many hours at my window overlooking the garden, listening to the cheerless notes of some lovelorn bird.

This state of affairs seems to cause much imbalance in people. The noonday sun scorches the faces of travellers through the deserts. It slows down the gait of the camels. In their fields, the farmer's crops are laid waste, the boats of their ambitions and the dreams of the cow herders drown in the vortex of misfortune, so harsh is the heat. Lakes begin to run dry. Ample gardens once resplendent, in a thrice, lose their leaves and blooms and become bereft of foliage.

The scorching noonday sun burns up the clear springs of thousands, but it does not bring any harm to me.

It lends my beloved banana plants a fierce sheen. It brings to life unseen nuances of colour in the wings of the bulbul. The fiery rays of light cause the waters of ponds and streams to sparkle. People appear to me bathing in this glorious light.

It is not my concern if this noonday brings joy to others or not—for I long for its brilliance in my gardens, to make my bananas shine and to spend hours in such splendid light, listening to the dulcet tones of the bulbul.

Utopia of the Poets:

A message from a poet to other poets
Comrades, we are all like the bird who wanders these pathways, blind in the cruelty of evening. This thing, life has done this to us; her restless nature, her chaos has impinged on our precious inner bliss, without regard for its sanctity.

Join me in perpetuity. Let us together renounce this artificial world; falling prey no longer to her art of deception. The toxic respiration of her inhabitants is desiccating the festoons of our lives, the way autumn winds wither leaves.

They call us the worshippers of dreams. They can only taunt and jibe.

Do we not have enough to contend with? The Angel of Death could rend our very existence null and void with her terrifying grip.

This is why comrades, I say, let us go. Let us run from this place and find our own way. We could even begin our travels on a peaceful night in spring if you so please—just let us leave this place.

With neither rest as our object, nor any interest in placidity, indifferent to apathy, devoid of inertia, free of all worldly concerns and unencumbered by the cares of life; we shall set forth to prepare for our sacred pilgrimage.

Comrade, we will traverse even the most impenetrable deserts with the prowess of the mightiest of winds.

We will cross the purpled, lashing, endless oceans like rolling, dangerous thunder clouds. We shall navigate picayune fields, interminable deserts, inhospitable valleys, unsafe, and deserted waterways alike like fearless beasts.

From across the moon, we will abscond like angels mad for journeying, flying stealthily towards the firmament, hidden from prying human eyes by the dark cloak of night.

We shall cross the sun too, like an aeroplane flies past a volcano, unconcerned.

By this time, comrade, at this point of our passage, we will begin to feel true liberation coursing through our veins and the power of absolute sovereignty.

Along the way if we meet celestial beings, we will ask them where our Utopia lies. The space where Spirit is liberated and hearts are granted felicity; where the inhabitants feel your pain when they speak to you.

On this odyssey, we shall meet the honey bees searching the hinterlands for only the most succulent flora. We shall put our plan before them:

Where is our realm, Bees? The place where the very earth holds the sacred foot-
prints of Liberty.
We shall seek the counsel of the bulbuls too, to answer the question:
In which direction does our land lie? The place where angels bathe their spark-
ling bodies on the banks? The place where the dulcet notes of the birds
sound out the sweetness of life in poetry. Pianos sing while the spirits
play the music of mysteries on their lutes.
We will appoint the cumulus clouds of spring as our voice. With them and
only with them shall we set out in search of our true nation. Where
the clouds are iridescent like the wings of a fairy and wrought with
fine artistry like the leaf, the petal, the flower—all equally light and
dancing.
The secrets of progress are hidden in the winning songs of the farmers in that
land, whose herds are brimming with milk and orchards plenteous
with pomegranates.
In this place, the luminary of our lived lives shall in the empyrean poetic,
never set.
This is our eternal abode.
And this is what people have believed to be the Olympus of the poets.

The Heat

So very black, the carpenter bees are back to their repetitious work courting the kanwal flower. The crimson beaks of the wild green parrots clutch mulberries. Fields that were verdant atop the mountains are shrivelled to almond-coloured grasses.

Serenaded by honey bees, luscious flora in the depths of the forest, give up nectar. Down in the valleys, the goats too receive nourishment from the earth.

Those halcyon days of summer that glitter in the visions of poets are here, hot and full like Arabian musk. These are the days of new light being born. We are surrounded by a waterfall of golden illuminations, as if the celestial floodgates have opened wide.

From the fathomless indigo sky, this light pours—the ocean, mountain ranges, forests—the entire land as far as the eye can see; everything, everything is illuminated.

The halcyon days of summer have arrived. Again the sun will ascend and sparkle. The hares shall dance enraptured. See how the star of day glitters in a sky just as crystalline as it is blue—the way light might tremble in the eye of a fawn.

Exuberant and zealous shafts of shimmering sunlight glissade off the opalescent wings of the birds like fine crystals of ice melting.

The halcyon days of summer are here. Light radiates in waves drowning us.

Treatise against Eternal Death Inspired by a Shadow

Do not speak to me in dirge-like tone of our ultimate dissolution or that we
   have come here on this earth to disappear. That is not the poetic
   truth I have gleaned, nor have the hands of annihilation frightened
   me by their touch. I hold no fascination for the yawning charm of
   the grave and its dire infinity of aloneness. My heart-mind remains
   perpetually connected to the hallowed ground of immortality; they
   share an eternal light.
So I don't want to hear that each and every breath I take, day in and day out is
   leading me to drown in a deathless hush of all future breaths.
And neither do you need to alert me to the horrors of the day to come that
   I may lose all hope. I do not need you to state darkly that we are all
   just here to meet with our own demise. I cannot place my belief in
   this. Surely, I have not been gifted eyes only for barbarous Death to
   shut them permanently.
I have not been given a beating heart brimming with impressions, sentiments,
   and passions just for the unfriendly hand of dissolution to stop
   them in their tracks as the needle-like hands of a clock might.
If death has any power it will only be able to affect the separation of my
   spirit from my body and my body from my spirit, much like a rose
   separated from its branch.
The following does not strike me as an odd thing to declare:
Death shall not overcome the aurora of my spirit with engulfing darkness.
It will never shut down my powers of sight.
It shall not plunder my sense of self, a living mass of emotions, thoughts and
feelings. Death shall turn back, confounded upon facing me.
Listen closely:
Stars coruscate with aplomb in the sky on a hot night.
Even the most insignificant bit of cloud can obscure their light, rendering
   the beams invisible on earth, and yet their innate nature to shine
   does not suffer in the slightest. They remain unchanged; a perpetual
   dance of light.
My spirit shall reside forevermore smiling out behind the stars. Let the open
   sky of my life be marred by death clouds and my body vanish from
   sight like the stars obscured by cloud. My spirit will remain unchanged; a light amongst lights rejoicing.
No. Do not sing me your dirges of our inescapable dissolution.

Existence

There is a certain sound that is emitted when the clouds of autumn collide with the mountains.
'What is existence?' they enquire of Nature. I hear secrets concealed in the formidable crashes of the ocean billows.
I too habitually enquire: 'What is this existence?'
Yes, existence. Your name contains within it burning pain.

I hear the bulbul somewhere far off. I imagine her seated in the sultanate of air and sky, expressing her sentiments regarding this life. Even so, I am unable to discern a definitive answer. Why should I ascend life's undiscovered heights and traverse her inhospitable banks? Why should I go at it alone?

When the dead blooms of the jasmine struggle to come back to life in the winds of spring and the softest light of the moon causes a certain sweetness to be born in the pomegranate, I ask:

'What is the meaning of this quickening of life.
What is it, that we call existence?'

I regret to say, answer comes there none.

The sun has set behind the henna shrubs, the sound and fury of the organ too winds down. We are beset by silence. Melancholia descends. I find the atmosphere quite cheerless. It feels like it may be time for angels to alight.

And I remain, in my state of contemplation on existence.

Ma Chérie Écoute

Listen girl. I say this with love. You must alter the manner in which you present yourself to the world.

You are too unguarded. Your mannerisms are disagreeable, giving the world the wrong impression.

Look. A doe appears innocuous but if she sees her fawns injured or hurt in any way she rallies like a She-lion.

As for you, your utterances are guileless and are misleading. They cause people to misunderstand you.

The bulbul's song is imbued with an innate sweetness, soothing hearts, but she is also capable of causing a person to experience bitterness with her woeful notes.

I hope your sentences laden with their natural goodness do not misrepresent you in the hearts of people.

For these reasons, my beloved girl—change your demeanour post-haste.

Missing Pages from the Book of Life

A time now irretrievable

From behind mottled curtains of cloud, an autumnal morning regarded Creation. The combination of cloud and dust gave the weather license to be reckless. A dreadful silence descended broken only by the undulating winds. Over on the coast, a simoom rising.

On the towering trees in the cemetery, doves cried. Parrots of the sea and mountain myna screamed out from ocean passageways. The winds whipping up forced the mightiest of almond and fig trees to sway and bend, kiss the ground and rise again with each gust. Other songs were layered into this soundscape; the songs of the fishermen and wayfarers. Everything spelt tragedy.

On the stairwell leading down into my garden, I observed silently the leaves and petals of the roses, ravaged by the simoom. Before my eyes, the ocean billows crashed into the horizon. I succumbed to the past. One memory in particular, heady and electric, yet so very bittersweet . . . my heart felt made of the most fragile of glasses, cracking to bits upon recalling it. I sensed my spirit unable to bear this burden of unbidden memory, parting from my body as I saw an image emerge of you and I, five years earlier.

Do you remember? Us riding like princesses of Baghdad through the gardens of nobility on the hunt for deer and rabbits. It was our hair that was responsible for our famed beauty. Our curls billowed as we rode astride the finest Arabian horses.

Our eyes of jet, saturated with the requisite eastern modesty, yet seeking out ardently the kill we sought in the deepest recesses of the bush. This bittersweet pull of yesteryear haunts me, as I relive those moments. We were wild, so wild for the hunt.

On the banks of streams, we caught fish, barefoot, out of sight of your father. Blue satin ribbons held up our hair, rippling in the wind. We were as the wild deer charging through the gardens.

I admit, it is impossible for me to reconcile this mournful day in the present with those, the days of euphoria.

On Thought

He can often be found scaling celestial heights and scouring the depths of the
sky, seeking out its secrets. Other times he struggles to comprehend
mundane matters here on the ground, just as he is unable to scale a
simple wall. How is it then he can effortlessly ascend a mountain as
imposing as Everest?

When the Spirit, naturally inclined to silent contemplation is meditating in
peace in some wilderness of Mind's creation, he appears, presenting
the sound and fury of wartime, in an effort to wilfully create disturbance. It works.

If our bodies were beset by the arrows and swords of a foe, he could well
be miles away from the noise of the battlefield on some abandoned
highway laughing his head off.

But by the same token, his sight can be so keen as to spot the gleam of the
hidden ears on gold itself. Other times, you could throw the most
magnificent of gemstones right at him and those blinded eyes with
pellucid surfaces would not see it.

Concealment

'The darkness outside is hellish! But wait . . . look here . . . is that the moon rising? It appears a little sickly. Perhaps we can sit together in contemplation on the eternal questions? Life . . . what is it? Love . . . what is the face of such a thing?'

To be honest, I was fed up that evening of the solitude of my room. The candles were burning. I was singing ghazals to myself when my girlfriend opened a window looking out onto the garden.

For some reason though, her request alarmed me. I replied noncommittally, 'I prefer not-knowing'. It took me a while, but I joined her at the window. As I gazed out, the incredibly finespun and tender moonlight became apparent in my vision. So faint and silvery it was.

As always, I was aware of the bittersweet tang of a seemingly lush moment.

The moon rose soundlessly. It was like watching a soul slowly separated from this earthly body.

I felt enveloped in an ethereal reality, like an angel was playing a harp on the beach. Such delicate, cool breezes and another sound coming in . . . an organ being played softly?

A strong fragrance from the orange blossoms enveloped me, like the perfume emanating from the garb of fairies of the waters. Reflections of rose leaves trembled in the moonlight—hallowed spirits roaming free everywhere.

I remained silent. As a corpse.

'You balk at the examination of life. I do understand irony. A butterfly sits on a bloom and lo and behold its petals are propagated but if a nightingale just looks at it from afar, the flower dies. But my dear soul—have you not contemplated this: In the depth of Midwinter when people are shivering in the cold of December, huddled around fires, that luminous object exalted by poets rises in the night sky and all comes alive in diamond light. But it makes no difference whether entire valleys are sparkling in this light or towering mountains . . . for there is no-one there to see them. I ask you then, does the beauty vanish like the brilliance of a gemstone that sinks in the ocean? I mean, does anyone know how many dazzling pearls lie in the abyss of the ocean or how exquisite they are? Yes, it may well be that when one who has knowledge of these things is born then the hidden may yet become the revealed, and the concealed come into the light. And by the same token, it can be said that when these round marble-like pearls become adornments

for necks then their innate beauty is brought out . . . I consider life to be just like this'.

On that note, my friend ended her treatise.

Now I'm not sure why I felt inflamed with anger. I gazed in compassion at my inexperienced hands, fragrant with sandlewood. I pitied myself in that moment.

'I do not wish to lift the veil off the face of existence. I prefer things to remain a mystery', was my resolute reply.

Prayer

On a morning that felt especially sanctified, his head was drooping. It was not yet sunrise. The moon still smiled on in the navy sky of night. In my field of vision from the window I could see the shadows of beatified spirits marring the pale moon light.

But his head was drooping.

Those who offered the early morning prayer had set off for their places of devotion. Sunlight appeared through the fronds of the date palms. Outside my room of worship, a small but effective creature remained rapt in song for a while before leaving.

His head remained down.

A celestial being was flying in the fresh morning breeze. Her complete absorption in prayer inspired him to smile.

His head rose as if of its own volition.

An Autumn Leaf

The vagaries of wind and rain had caused the visage of the rose to vanish. Her leaves were withered and browning.

I kept watch alone in an unoccupied corner of the courtyard on a fervourless afternoon in autumn. I saw a leaf, fatigued by seasonal strife taking a breath on the wizened grass. What I was to witness was rather harrowing.

The leaf tried to gather strength and rise up briefly only to fall right back, defeated onto the grass. It was painful to watch.

I wanted to speak to it as a friend would and advise it to stop trying to win a losing battle:

'Fate has not exactly bestowed you with tranquillity, little leaf. First you experienced yellowing, then were battered and the final blow was when you were knocked off the tree. I do not think there is peace to be found anywhere for you now. Why do you try to travel elsewhere? This journey you wish to embark on won't restore your felicity. The lustre of youth never returns. If you keep attempting movement, it is almost certain this ill-fated flight of yours will land you in a stream, to be drowned in the water. Or the hostile winds could carry you off to a city street only to be trod underfoot by a callous passer-by.

I worry that any further journeys might create more problems for you. You could land in some window of a house and a child mistaking you for a butterfly may wish to play with you. What then?

I say you should remain where you are. Hold fast. Your path is pre-assigned.

Remain where you are and wait for the time to come that I too long for.

Dearest saffron leaf, your story really does resemble mine in so many ways. I too am like a dry and yellowing leaf on the date tree of the world that autumn's cruel winds have displaced, keeping me from the enjoyment of life, from hope. I too remain in a state of discomfort—my patience being constantly tested.

The difference is, I am not reckless like you. I am laying here where the far-reaching hands of the powers that be threw me.

And here, I wait for the same time to come as you do.

Come, my trusted friend, let us wait together, laying here, you and I in this desolate part of the garden and anticipate the coming spring'.

Simplicity

I must admit, I make no difference between the pure waters of a spring and the aged wine of the grape. What is the difference? Do tell. If you look closely, can you find any difference between the hues on the scales of those tiny fish in the lake and the light of the small, sweet stars twinkling on the horizon?

Have you felt the difference between the hot flickering of a fire and the soft drops of evening in the form of dew?

When the strings of your instrument are broken, how can you play the true raga of life?

Separation

It was not so long ago that gazing out of my window at the sea, cerulean like the sky, would lend a kind of order to my chaotic breathing. My hardened manner would soften and those around me would remark how my lips (usually so silent) would stay aglow with a rarefied smile. It is not so today.

The strange thing is that today, in the black and white of the billows, my heart is beating in time with their every movement.

I wonder, Lordy, what secret workings are these?

On any other day, spying one of those majestic ships creates an instant turn of colour on my face to the blush of happiness and my eyes of black coruscate like blazing stars. Usually, I exhale great big sighs of jealousy and envy at the excellent fortune of those travellers in those ships. Today, I say, this is not so.

Today . . . I am afraid of those sails and grow pale at the sight of them.

On any other day, the electric light reminds me of the natural shine of fate. This is not that day.

Today. . . I see them as demons that roam the deserts and I prefer the darkness of a starless night over these lights.

Here's the thing, buddy. Here's the thing: this time you and I will be pulled apart. O Lordy. Yes, believe me. We will be separated.

Uff what a stunning display! The ship is pulling out from the docks, slowly being separated from the traveller. The soul is pulled out of the body. And . . .

And the world behind you appears as if a body without the spirit.

That Unforgettable Morning

Finally, morning broke. It was to be memorable. For my attire, I donned a viridescent ocean-blue dress inlaid along the sides with sea shells and artificial pearls. The season of colour that was upon us lent my face a natural blush and I could not stop smiling. I was aware that my jet-black hair too complemented the colouring on my face. I tied it back with a golden ribbon so it would not vex me during the heady hours of waiting that lay ahead.

I glanced out of the window. Before me the sea crashed out wave upon wave. It felt for all the world as if those white-crested, azure breakers were determined to knock heads with the sky. In this endless lazuline watery flood, I searched for your ship which was meant to arrive any moment. Yes, any moment, Lord.

I looked over into the garden.

The domestic was breaking up dried fruit to accompany the afternoon meal. She looked up at me sceptically. I tried to look away and perhaps conceal this smile, like a talisman, this smile whose luminosity I could not control. It was no use; the smile only grew larger. In fact, that morning my soul felt engulfed in eternal laughter.

Along with the girl laying out lunch, the birds seemed to be singing teasing songs in the box and jujube trees, while the scarlet roses appeared amused by my untoward restlessness, gossiping amongst themselves.

I could hear songs of arrival and welcome in the waters of the fountain, as if everything under the sun was in harmony, offering me congratulations on your return.

Indeed, by the window, the winds sounded like sweet notes of an organ. I felt rapt in a world of dream and story.

On this morning, taking measure of my intense absorption in waiting and complete state of dissolution, the girl went and got out the largest silver vases and filled them with narcissus flowers, placing them in every corner of the house and all along the window ledges.

My faithful dog too sat in the doorway in wait for the beloved guest who was meant to arrive.

Seeing all this ceremony and activity, I got suspicious. Was the shadow of dawn breaking in the heavens being cast over my charming little house?

I was awaiting a ship. Yes, your ship

Some time lapsed, soft sunlight turned the mighty ocean rollers gold. In the distance, when I wasn't expecting to see it, there it was at last, the sail of your ship.

Still far—so very far away from the shore. It was as if a picture of me was swimming in the billows on the water and wave by wave was trying too, to reach the shore.

At last, your ship pulled into the harbour.

The universe transformed into a musical instrument, with no other utterances at its disposal besides a vocabulary of joy and songs of sheer delight.

That morning, that oh so unforgettable morning has stayed with me to this day. Beautiful traveller! Your ship finally docked on eastern shores.

The Fantastic Luck of Travellers

I awake to the unending dream of my life at dawn, restless and every morning I hear the ocean without limits, roaring.

Come nightfall, I fall asleep to the same powerful sound. I am a castaway on these desolate eastern shores, where the sun burns relentlessly like red-hot coals for twelve months of the year. I am cursed to live out my days in silence.

Off on the horizon, I watch ships pass with their grand sails. It appears to me as if a mighty angel is moving, arms of light wide open, on a thin, blue line towards the wilds. Often my restless eyes remain fixated on those whiter than white sails, till I can see nothing else.

The ships leave the harbour calm and graceful on the great depths of the sea eventually vanishing. Sitting on the untraversed and desolate sands glittering in the sunlight adorned with milky, opalescent sea shells, I lament. I am so jealous of the fantastic fortune of travellers.

Defeated! Lord I must ask you this:

Is freedom only written in the stars for travellers?

When the world is too much with me and I feel reduced, when the task of the completion of my diminished dreams scares me off, when the betrayals and disappointments of those I thought to be my friends, wound me deeply and I wish for death . . . and my world seems to have become a target for mishap and misfortune, I wonder:

Whose brow bears the lines that spell out, REPRIEVE.

You, traveller unfettered by the disturbance of the world, immune to its constant tug of war; you remind me of a lucky fish swimming in the waters of freedom which to me sounds like bliss.

Certainly, your face appears to me glowing with inner joy and your forehead seems etched with lines that speak of liberation.

You come and go as you please—traversing distances unimaginable—conquering the seven seas, passing by new islands never discovered, surveying elegant settlements from the coast as you voyage on . . . released from worldly reflection and blissfully unaware of the imbalances of existence.

I wonder if what you search for so endlessly with a smile on your face, is in fact the most vital of all your breaths, that you left on some abandoned shore.

I ask you, is it true that in this world liberation and insouciance has been apportioned only to you and your fantastic luck? Do you by any chance have a secret contrivance that can magically transform this entire world into a vast sea of roaring waves and we, set sail on the sturdy constructions of our lives as travellers like you and find the Utopia we too seek.

Your Call in the Wild; the Imaginings of a Girl Cutting Wheat in the Fields

I see you, in the wars, becoming a gleaming sword. I wonder what you're doing right now.

On a bitterly cold morning in November, wearing a threadbare shawl, I was in the fields reaping wheat while the star of morning sparkled. The silver moonlight laid out a delicate tapestry of light on the verdure of the fields. The crisp and zealous northern winds were playing fast and loose with my clothing. The nightingales flying through the fields of corn, sitting in the guava trees warbled with gusto.

I wonder, dearest love what you're doing right now. I see you, in the wars, becoming a gleaming sword.

* * *

Today the ocean breakers are crashing on the shore violently. The strong fragrance of henna flowers is intent on assailing my senses. The perfect notes of the songs of farmers are competing for my attention. But all of this is to no avail. There is not one instrument in this orchestra of whole mellifluous notes that will separate me from thoughts of my lover and share my attention.

At dusk, when I am returning home through the fields, the sunlight sets my deep sapphire dress glowing, turning it iridescent, radiating all the colours of the universe. The musical peals of the laughter of children and the gorgeous singing of the night birds spread on the airwaves of evening.

None of these things really interest me though. For after sunset, there is an otherworldly raga, a tenor of joy that I listen to that seems to me to be the most supreme sound of all sounds in the universe and that is your call in the wild.

Young Ascetic

What allure lies in the rocks of the Himalayas separating you from your well-wishers.

The heat of eastern climes is known to take lives and wear away at souls. Does your body which seems made of marble not feel it?

I see you. In the forests, when the sun high overhead us in the azure sky is blazing like a giant cinder from Hell and the shadow cast by the mighty oak lands on my sundial. Even the roaring ocean has offered up her waters to melt like iron.

I see you even when the goats, troubled by the scorching temperatures flee to the mountain streams, unable to stop drinking. I see when the ground shimmers like the swords of warriors; you sit on the skin of a lioness rapt in your prayer beads, with ash and earth rubbed on your body.

I see you on the most lightless of monsoon nights that would terrify most when after the unrelenting sun, the bedlam of the waters of the monsoon mistral rains creates craters in the ground. Mountain caves, desolate valleys, and the wild sea causeways are plunged into darkness while gale-force winds ravage the land like the trumpeting call to arms of war.

You have offered up the best days of your life, your youth, your vigour to contemplation and devotion. Night after night you remain seated in some silent ruins or uninhabited corner, worrying your prayer beads as if you are curled up on a cosy winter's evening with the stories of your favourite author.

I wonder what it is you have seen here, in the heart of the Himalayas, in this specific part of Asia where the crests of the mountain range converse with the indigo sky.

What eternal fire there burns so bright and vari-coloured? What spark has been ignited that transports you atop a tall mountain, ready to fall on the fire, not caring if your corpus burns or melts?

The Sleep of the Bulbul

What darkness envelopes us. The bulbul is slumbering and so the music of the universe has died down to a halt.

Sensing this, the crustacean has wrapped up his heart-rending song. The wind, similarly inspired, has decided to catch a few breaths on the desolate shore.

The trees are murmuring in conversation with each other. A deep stillness engulfs the spring. The bulbul has closed her eyes and so Nature is lost in dream.

The poet is ever watchful. An insomniac. Restless, unable to sleep, witnessing the night full of gravitas.

From the east, a sirocco has infiltrated the rose bush, with petals and flowers strewn on the ground, crushed underfoot by passers-by. He stoops, whispering to a crimson rose. The rose sways from side to side, her petals moving faster in the wind, never opening her eyes, so strong is the grip of sleep.

The winds have disturbed the bulbul. She turns over in her sleep and awakens, rubbing her eyes—having only half-slept. She sets off into the mountains, in the still, sombre darkness of night to find the crimson rose.

But she will not find her. In this life, we all fall prey to deception. The rose, her eyes closed, found herself simply swinging in a reverie on her branch, not knowing she was being carried off in the wind. Just as the bird too is unknowing.

She sighs. Two teardrops fall on the rose bushes. She cries for her sleep and laments her loss. Perhaps like the poet, the bulbul too is destined for insomnia and her life too is an extended sigh. Perhaps if we wait, those two teardrops will render a crimson rose when spring arrives. Perhaps we have uncovered one of the great secrets of the creation of our material world:

The rose is born of two teardrops of a bulbul.

Raison D'Etre

She placed her long, elegant fingers on the strings of the saz, as delicate fingers of light from the candle flame too played on it.

'Look how nature has gifted a raison d'etre to everything she creates. Come closer, look how the strings of the saz are restless to be played, for a song. They remember well their origins. And how rapidly the journey of the autumn sun ends.

See how on a winter's morning little rivers sing with such verve and gusto, just as in the solitude of night, the owl speaks up in heart-rending tones amidst the desolate trees and uninhabited expanses of walls.

They all know well their true nature. See how a ghost will always recognize the Angel of Death even in darkness.

Nature has assigned everything its own special work; a true pre-occupation.'

Her sigh so deep appears to come from a place of great disappointment. 'What my raison d'etre is . . . I still don't know.'

A deathly silence falls upon us, on this evening in autumn when it is easy to feel unhappy. From deep in the valleys, the continuous yearning crowing of roosters, echoes.

* * *

In the mist-laden haze of evening, the autumnal sun was sinking slowly on the horizon. The inclement weather caused the smile of the bulbul to vanish. On evenings such as this, the world seems an instrument completely devoid of music or a verse without a note. At that moment, life appeared a joyless story or a dream with no interpretation.

She was mourning being unable to remember her own essential occupation. She had forgotten the songs of her spirit.

That evening, that autumnal evening—lightless, dismal—when life appeared a voyage devoid of meaning.

Gazing in this dark mood out of the window, I saw beside the wall of the garden the small delicate, bloom of a water lilly, dancing upon the waters of the pond in the chilly wind. It was inhaling the breath of life with each movement.

Something came to me. I said to her:

'Is living life in itself not an albeit difficult but valid pre-occupation?'

Upon hearing this, a smile lit up her face like the fiery tones of the autumn sun.

An Afternoon in Summer

Under the mulberry tree, such restlessness in the way that bird is flapping its wings! And in the guava tree both a crow completely ignorant of the rules of music and wild green parrots are simultaneously emitting such truly hideous screams!

It appears, it is afternoon.

Monsoon

Those days have doubled back in their tracks and arrived. They awaken my dreams.

The tumultuous monsoon season weather in this hot eastern clime I inhabit holds great power. Once upon us, the succulent, glittering jewel-like drops of rain and monsoon clouds purpled with water, awaken the influx of memories of incidents past, like the strains of forgotten poetry.

You may well find yourself rooted to the spot, hours pass, you wouldn't know, propelled as you are into the realm of dream, watching images of old and hearing melodies of yore. For a spirit inclined to fancy, it is a time of intensity and passion.

It has often been the case during some monsoon season or the other, that a chapter of an unfinished novel has come to me or I have figured out the personality of a person in a story, but before I get a chance to jot these ideas down on the page, the season changes and the rain travels onward to distant shores. These thoughts of a writer's craft, also disappear with the clouds. Only the architect of the universe holds the knowledge of where they go.

I will not be able to savour any of these ideas till the next season of rain comes around again, to remind me.

* * *

When the winds bring the fragrance of the approaching monsoon season the nightingale on the cedar tree begins her songs of rain and the ultramarine of the sky is reflected on the ocean waves and finally when my writing room is enrobed in a dark curtain of cloud, then and only then, word for word, those thoughts, those stories will come back to life in my mind.

Other people say that a heart that feels so deeply and an intellect that concocts stories may well be a gift to be grateful for. But Lord knows, today this feeling heart of mine is the sole reason there is a total absence of peace inside me today.

Fate is in bloom for those who, like stones battered by the ocean breakers or like mountains immoveable, can live unphased. The winds of zeitgeist, gusting sometimes hot, sometimes cold leave them unaffected.

They can appreciate the soft, undulations of a field of wheat in the breeze, but remain unmoved if that same field were to be overrun by the cruelty of thorns. The events of the past are easily forgotten.

I on the other hand have no such good fortune.

My memory chooses to secretly harbour fragments of tales from times—I have no idea why—and it is during occasions meant to hold only happiness or moments when joy should come easy that it chooses to reveal things that dissolve every thought in the potent poison of a python.

What then is this gift I have been so blessed with? Is this the empathetic heart my friends are filled with pride for? I implore you who sustain our existence! Enlighten me.

* * *

Listen! It was during the rains and all through the morning like the train of thought of a poet, unbroken, glitter-rain was falling from the sky.

I was surveying the view from the window of my library, with binoculars while my memory was engaged in turning the pages of a few years before, to some accomplished life I had. I say again, how I lament this soul of mine and its worship of fancy.

The window was open. The wild sea was riotous with breakers and in the aquamarine depths of these monsoon waves I could see, like pearls scattered on the waters, fragments of the narrative of my life.

I opened the door and stepped out into the garden.

The clouds no longer in a rain-state had expanded. I was standing under a young guava tree. My heart was overcome. Time, lost was too much with me and the song of life was clearly being played on the lute of Time. In the trees, wild green parrots were throwing the remains of guavas down, in petulance.

Racing towards the sea, clouds were scattering, so purple. I could smell the dampness of the rains on the wind. Black beaks glittering, crows were carrying twigs to build their nests hopping from tree to tree. Along the pathways of the gardens, my peacocks and rabbits were engaged in ritual dances like ancient African tribespeople.

The universe appeared a boat, sailing on a river of contentment and bliss. It was all it was, but dearest my long-entombed desires were trying to come back to life, gasping for breath and my soul was wandering, lost in some forgotten valleys.

It is true. Worshippers of dream and souls affected disproportionately by the small trials of life, shall neither experience an exalted state of joy nor a soothed heart.

Why then do you envy my state? Sweet one, a soul that remembers every little detail of life does not live a life worth envying. You must now accept this. You are wrong.

* * *

Afternoon. The footpaths are still and the alleyways lay deserted. Not a wanderer in sight. Every direction holds silence except for the lilting refrains reaching me from afar of the reed flute being played by a tired goatherder, dancing with the rain-drenched breezes.

On this mournful afternoon after the rains, from yonder the unremitting lament of the rooster.

* * *

I returned to my library. I contemplated the truth of my own experience; contentment and calm get lost in the winds in the season of rain. Once more, I returned to my window and counted the ocean waves rising and falling. I journeyed back to dream and story.

All that was left for me was an imaginary world

The Spirit of Cupid

Last night, I left the window to my chamber of dreams open. I felt as if just behind me, a benign shadow stood smiling as under the antique pallor of the moon, my heart seemed to dissolve.

The truth is often obscured by people who consider the accounts of poets as merely pleasant dreams to linger in or barely formed reflections of the mystical words of the great poet, Omar Khayyam.

I hear the music of the sky singing a raga of the winds. There is a melody that has spread in every direction. I hope you understand what I mean, my friends.

This is actually what I hear.

The kingdom of dreams may have an angel, a lover of music, playing the organ. On such a night, sparkling and calm, it could be a sprite of the sea emitting this music that causes the very solidity of the heart to be challenged.

I have heard that behind these mountains, there is a tortured yogi who plays the flute. My Maker, I submit to you, there is so much pain in this raga.

Last night, I left the window to my chamber of dreams open. It felt as if just behind me, a benign shadow stood smiling as under the antique pallor of the moon, my heart seemed to dissolve. The winds carried pure music.

Those who require explanation might well surmise that this music was coming from the fine springtime clouds perched atop the lush green mountains, engaged in a hymnal to the fine, fine weather.

Or . . .

Are these the cries for help of someone who is laden with the pain of abandonment—perhaps the screams of a disenchanted poet? I fret that this sound is the collective groaning of the weak, the powerless.

Some might say, this is the lament to the Adored One of all that is alive, asking for something, troubled and wary of the tribulations of existence.

Or . . .

What if the sounds are that of the solitary philosophical joke in the sweet, vexing arias of the crickets, causing shivers in my soul?

Last night, I left the window to my chamber of dreams open. It felt as is just behind me, a benign shadow stood smiling as under the antique pallor of the moon, my heart seemed to dissolve.

Some might say, these sounds are the image of the King of Dreams who is smiling over my sleep. But what if this is the remembrance of the Divine casting shadows on my forgetful state? What if this is the very spirit of Cupid, watching the sleep of poets in the dead of night, through the celestial windows?

Reader, it was through the sweet tones of the organs and the voice like a waterfall, that the spirit of Cupid was asking me questions about a life of poetry—I lament my own ignorance.

I peered out at the valley below the window at the olive and guava trees inclined to appear dark and saw glimpses of their green branches over which the moon appeared to be running with some speed.

And the valley was aglow like the forehead of an angel. And yes, a song was upon the winds.

I know others might say it may be a traveller playing his flute, or the bugle of a soldier shaking up the atmosphere of the jungle.

But what if these sly waves are tickling and tickling and tickling, the sea in order to make her laugh.

What if the sound I hear is in fact, the ocean guffawing with joy, swords laughing—there is a bittersweet pain in my heart—so effective is this song.

You, whom I worship. You are the song of a tortured bulbul that sits wings
spread in the moonlight on a solitary delicate branch of the
tree of tristesse and in those moments pregnant night, still and silent, sings its song of tragedy.

And it is the shade of her wings that people call the spirit of Cupid! The spirit
of Cupid who waits for the absolute stillness of moonlit nights to
smile over poets.

Reader—Now you must sleep. Look outside.

It is later than you think.

Fascination

On the ground, there is a continuous state of motion and activity while in the sky, she is screeching and whipping across the sky—the Wind. All around me there is always a state of perpetual disturbance. In the jungles, the beasts fight for their daily survival.

In the oceans, the fish too are entangled in the tussle of life. All around me there is unrest.

I stand, separated from all these things in my own centre of silence.

Addressing the Poet

Dear Writer, I wonder if an autumnal faery's arm brushed against your thoughts; what other explanation could there be for the immaculate inspiration you received?

Ray of Pure Light

In the earliest part of morning, she arrives past the clouds over the mountain range, as if a celestial being has brought a message down from the stars.

Then her trajectory shifts down from the mountains onto the tempestuous, roaring ocean waves and she becomes an enraptured fairy dancing on islands made of pearls.

She keeps moving on, reaches the desert, glinting and gleaming on the swords of the Bedouin. Her light like drops of blood of the enemy— sometimes a glimmer of bravery in the eye of a warrior, at other times, the desire for victory sparkling on their weapons.

* * *

And then it is time for evening and the world becomes like a small child rubbing her eyes ready for sleep. With the advent of the appointed time, the Sun too is happy to retire.

Swords slumber in their sheaths.

She ascends once more the mountains, returning along the same well-trodden path. She vanishes, leaving traces of a prayer.

I am left feeling as if a truly sacred spirit has risen to the celestial throne room, bowing her head to the ground, upon reaching.

When I Get the Blues

I get the blues sometimes and head out into the fields to lift my spirits. It is a mystery to me, Lordy Lord how these people, these people of the world appear so happy, busy in their work when I, I got the blues so bad.

Everyday those working in the fields head out into the green, lush expanses and they croon ragas of joy. So happy they are with harvesting, cutting, and reaping.

Everyday I see how the southerly wind toys with abandon, like a lover with the branches of henna shrubs, not quite trees, spreading the glorious fragrance of the darling henna buds in the pure air of the forest.

I see slender birds crafted like delicate sculptures, their voices, raised in tumultuous song, on the desolate shores of the roaring sea. Their music, rapturous, talking of love and grandeur.

I say Lord—when will I too be blessed with such freedom.

When I hear the young girls too singing in the fields in the fracas of a morning in the monsoons.

When I hear the song of the boatman, as he sings on a still moonlit night, or when the triumphant sounds of a soldier's bugle knock me out of my reveries setting off the deep restlessness, in every crevice of my fleeting state of calm . . . frustrated, I question you, Nature:

Why am I bereft of joy?

I sense a restless desire for freedom in every string of my harp, in the false sense of tranquillity, not tranquillity at all, but a volatile and frenetic thing. I question you, Nature.

Why can I not be one pure, happy note?

In the tall shadows of noon, I marvel at the calm of the cattle as they nourish themselves with emerald grasses.

And I marvel at the goat-herders high up on the mountains as they sit under the protection of dense foliage and beatific valleys playing the reed flute so tenderly.

My heart questions my existence. It wants to sing a raga like all these beings, a raga resembling felicity. It wants to envision a euphoric dream of harmony.

She does not answer—Nature. Like the women in the hieroglyphs of Misr, still and unmoving, she stares at my countenance and answer comes there none.

During the Monsoon, the Westering Sun

All the shadows of the world have sequestered themselves in the clouds. Light and dark have merged into one. The winds, waves, and earth are silent.

The distant sounds of echoing sea-birds singing mingle with the water-laden air, echoing over the abandoned shores.

Every now and again, I hear the haunting sounds of the smallest of ocean waves like angels singing in a dream.

Slowly, little by little the sun is surely drowning. Only you, my dearest friend, would understand how this is a metaphor for my old desires as they take their last breath with it.

The sun will be re-born again but I am not so fortunate as my dreams are dead and gone forever.

Everywhere darkness is falling fast and the whereabouts of all light in the Universe is untraceable.

Winter evening, this black evening spread upon the world is trying to embrace it in her arms.

See, now 'tis over. The sun has set. Sunken into the thick monsoon clouds. The world now lightless sits on the banks of the river hoping to pass the night there like a weary traveller with nowhere else to go.

I wish it a good night.

The Sea

In reply to a poem by Canadian poet Frederick George Scott's poem 'Little River'.

He who says there is nothing on your shores knows nothing. The significance of those indigo billows of yours is one of the great, unexplained Mysteries. And your breezes are accomplished musicians calming us with their ragas. Somebody should ask the poet why the river should not meet the great sea? What does the river have on its shores that compares? Reeds and wild cypress trees under whose tall and dense growth the cruel hot air of the afternoon recklessly tries to knock heads about?

Or is it the dead leaves on the banks that sing mournful dirges in memory of their youth and vigour in spring? And the frightening songs and tuneless cacophony of the crustaceans in the dead of night. At the extremities of the 'Little River', lies overgrowth in which the dangerous hissing of snakes burns in the winds, like some barbaric chant.

No true poet could find peace here. There is no contemplation on Life's riddles and wonders here. There is no way to meditate on lost esoteric know-ledge here—on the contrary!

* * *

Dear Ocean! Your glittering shores and clarified air has held a romantic pla-cidity, an innate philosophical quietude since time immemorial. The kind of repose and stillness that both feeds the soul and the intellect. It is as if an an-cient story-telling angel, sits in your lashing and roaring breakers telling the story of Cupid and Psyche ad nauseum.

In my experience, those Divine rollers of yours hold compassion for story-tellers and love and affection for poets. The fate of poets is written on your shining, shell-strewn sands and perfectly formed stones.

I believe my star of destiny too must, in fact, scintillate in your sky-shores. Lovers of make-believe and those who worship dream receive benediction on your beaches.

I, myself, have known the magic and wonder of the sea since I was a child. You, my friend, and I should stay a while on the uninhabited beach and see if we too can come to recognize and know the great mysteries.

The Poet Wishes

I long for—

    The gathering of black clouds, who have taken in weighty nuggets of glitter, brazen across the indigo of the sky—and the tremble of one perfect, jagged line of electricity in the darkness—

But I thirst—

    For a glimpse behind the veil of black clouds where a world of fantasy and romance lies. I am convinced that the fragrant spring breeze causing a clamour when dishevelling the leaves on the branches of trees, is whispering secrets of her love—

And I yearn—

    To become one with the winds and know what the emerald leaves hear. Every evening at dusk, when I witness the sun, saffron and orange travel west and disappear, the same desire I have held onto for an age snaps her fingers at my core.

    I wish to accompany the sun for a little while concealed in the mysterious straits of the western skies and learn first-hand what keeps the sun so enthralled that she does not return till morning.

These, I declare to be my very deepest wishes.

The Long Way

The time had come when I could go no further. When I had set out initially, it had been morning. The flowers had a freshness about them and my spirit felt ebullient.

I was in such high spirits, I believed this fatigue could not touch me. This was a very human thought—limited in its grasp, futile and so, ultimately proven wrong.

For after some distance had been traversed, I felt as if even the orchards replete with grapes and the abundant fields of wheat were in accord with me, beset by weariness.

But what could I do? Even though I was tired, I kept moving forward.

Home was far away and I could see nothing around me but gravelly inhospitable ground and sky as far as the eye could see. And even if I was able to see any landmarks, they were the footprints of wild beasts roaming the forest at night, imprinted on the ground.

I was rudderless and so disoriented. I had no sense of anything except that my Spirit was plagued by an inexplicable weariness.

I tell you! It was a strange journey and such a long way to travel. While it is true that the journey was not without fascination, this existed simultaneously alongside fear and loathing. This was in fact the reason I had grown discontented with this junket.

I wished to reach the same point I had set out from in the morning before evening fall.

* * *

The sun began to drop lower and the grapevines appeared stolen away in an unconsciousness stupor. I could see my house now, at a short distance.

Evening set in with her spread of darkness and I was ascending the stairs to my home, at last to arrive at the final step.

I had arrived and if my spirit wasn't instantly uplifted! I once again, as if by magic, experienced the same ebullience of morning.

Flaxen Hair

A representational arrangement

On a particularly luminous evening, a sirocco blew through the vast expanse of sapphire sky, the sun effective as tropical suns are, adorning it. Walking past the rose garden of scarlet flowers, I alighted on the veranda. After perfunctorily examining some jasmine flowers scattered on the couch, I pulled back the curtains and arrived in the present.

The door into my friend's chambers was only half open so that I could just about make her out stood silently, facing a mirror taller than her, running a comb through her long, flaxen hair. She seemed quite alone, so alone.

Off to one side of the bedroom an elderly lady stood in front of the Japanese dresser folding my friend's clothes and putting them away.

The saffron light of the tropical sun was pettifogging the clouds imbued with orange hues. There was no sign of movement or life on my friend's features. Neither her lips nor her eyes belied any expression.

I could not contain my smile and tried not to laugh to give away my position. At the window, a bird overcome by the heat began to flap a wing in frustration. The sound, plangent, loud, breaking through the deep silence caused my friend to turn around swiftly. Her buttery sheath of hair obscured her vision but she soon spotted me. Her sombre mien soon broke out in laughter.

The door to the room opened soundlessly as the dowager attendant walked out gracefully.

Song

A prose poem

It is time. The sun has pulled curtains of night behind her and drowned herself in the horizon while humanity sleeps and the universe has been rendered unconscious by the embrace of repose. Sing a song, a song that invites my life to sparkle and coruscate like a sweet little star glinting behind a mighty mountain range, that is hidden from sight and laughing at itself.

A song that transforms my very spirit into such a flower that sits beneath fleshy emerald leaves under the protection of dense vines, unconcerned by the cruel fingers of the flower gatherer, living out its days in sheer contentment and tranquillity with pride in its existential condition.

Yes, a song just like this that fortifies my heart like the hard ground beneath us so that I see no difference between the thorny hard undergrowth of the acacia and the fine buds on the rose bush.

This is all so that when the fingers of the era pluck notes of anguish and sorrow or those of hope and mirth on the strings of my being, I remain nonplussed by their nuances, neither responsive to the sharp caustic tang of bitter acid, nor the cloying sweetness of halwa.

The Strings of the Instrument of Life Are Broken

How is it things can turn on a pin like a dream can, from beatific to pure terror—this is a real tragedy; our human story to despair of.

It is too painful to watch when a bud is trampled before it has a chance to bloom and by the same token how great is the misfortune of the flower that is given life on the winds of December; the lotus in the pond blooms, but an uncaring bought of rain causes it to drown in the very waters from which it was born.

The suffering heart that knows only melancholia, heightened desires and emotions has no right to unravel hope like some withered flower tossed upon the autumn winds.

Come spring, the elegant red flowers of the trumpet vine open themselves up on each and every branch to the brilliant rays of sunlight. In order to flourish and restore their glory they allow the vitality of the light to reach inside them and are keen to take in the reinvigorating air of spring.

In exactly the same way, I too have delivered light to each individual beat of the heart and it has now become fused within me like an electrical wave. During the monsoon season in sub-tropical climes, when the soft drops of rain water fall, the Earth accepts them immediately and becomes one with them. In exactly the same manner, I too have become one with the light of your spirit.

The outcome of this, however, has been one of being unsuccessful, wretched, and restless. Perhaps one day this world will be destroyed and I will be left standing here, defeated, on the threshold to Imagination, in the form of a fakir, with the demeanour of a beggar.

The centuries will roll on, new souls shall emerge to create a new world, only to return from where they came. Populated and uninhabited, uninhabited and populated will switch places ad nauseum and perhaps I, like a tornado, will continue to try ardently to reach the banks of my desires.

* * *

Every morning, that arrived in a blaze of light bringing with it the shine of burgeoning thoughts of hope would become unified with my feeble body, weak vitals, and restless spirit.

And every evening that brought the darkness with it to deliver the message of wretchedness, despair, misery, failure, and jealousy would cause my dreams to tremble and trample my vitality and my ambitions.

This has been occurring for an age and I fear it shall continue for several more.

The Advent of Evening

For My Sister Zakia Kazim Ali
Verse prose

Every evening by the saddened waters
Far removed from the habitations of the world

I sit in solitude watching the day drowning.

The water reaches my lap, singing
Golden clouds dance
On the edge of the waters of Lacrima
From the disruptive world, far removed

I sit in solitude watching the drowning day

Crystalline water laps at me and slips away on the rocks
The world in the black garb of grieving has arrived
To stand before me
And by the woeful waters
From the responsibilities of life, far removed

I sit watching the day as it drowns

And when the sky turns to black in lamentation
And mourning for its king
And when the leaves of the forest begin
To tremble from the intensity of their wailing.
And a terrifying raga emanates from the
wailing waters

I return, bringing back with me the impression
Of the day that has drowned
Aye, I have sat on this desolate rock, for an age watching the day die away at
the advent of evening, filling my heart with sighs and lamentation.

The Last Evening

I descended to the lower floor from my room.

You who possess all! That evening of 3 January was a dreadful one! The next morning the life of an innocent was to be sacrificed at the altar. In those separation-laden moments and anguish-ridden phrases of time, I wished to play a last raga on the lute, when I spied my uncle in a lustrous black evening jacket, appearing for all the world as if he was conscious of nothing, strolling in the garden.

Aye, I remember it well. His face was as white as a lotus in December and as devoid of vitality as a leaf in autumn. A certain air of dejection and despair was apparent. He tossed a cigar into the pots of roses, seeming worried and then withered into a couch by the narcissus flowers.

You know I am fond of composing poetry while breaking grapes off the vines. At that moment, I was searching for something to erase my sorrow. There were some vines nearby, so I busied myself with gathering grapes.

The sun was disappearing into the sea. It appeared as if a great python, nestling in the waves, was swallowing the sun. Darkness was catching up. The lotus flowers in the pond were gently stirring in the evening breeze. In the cedar and olive trees, the bulbuls slept. From afar, I spotted the window of your palace of dreams. Rays of electric light emanated from within, sparkling on the plants on the veranda. A veil of gloom had descended over the garden.

Aye, all of this made me feel like I was losing control.

I was contemplating life and all its suffering while continuing to pluck the grapes. The air felt cold as I drew breath. Such a restlessness had come over me over the last few hours that I was in a terrible state. I found a couch in the grape vines and sat down.

I knew, dearest, I knew that this was your very last evening.

W0230032

Belles-Lettres